The

BIPOLAR
HANDBOOK

FOR CHILDREN, TEENS, AND FAMILIES

THE
BIPOLAR
HANDBOOK

FOR CHILDREN, TEENS, AND FAMILIES

. . . .

Real-Life Questions
with Up-to-Date Answers

. . . .

Wes Burgess, M.D., Ph.D.

AVERY
a member of
Penguin Group (USA) Inc.
New York

Published by the Penguin Group
Penguin Group (USA) Inc., 375 Hudson Street, New York, New York 10014, USA •
Penguin Group (Canada), 90 Eglinton Avenue East, Suite 700, Toronto, Ontario M4P 2Y3, Canada
(a division of Pearson Canada Inc.) • Penguin Books Ltd, 80 Strand, London WC2R 0RL,
England • Penguin Ireland, 25 St Stephen's Green, Dublin 2, Ireland (a division of
Penguin Books Ltd) • Penguin Group (Australia), 250 Camberwell Road, Camberwell, Victoria 3124,
Australia (a division of Pearson Australia Group Pty Ltd) • Penguin Books India Pvt Ltd,
11 Community Centre, Panchsheel Park, New Delhi–110 017, India • Penguin Group (NZ),
67 Apollo Drive, Rosedale, North Shore 0632, New Zealand (a division
of Pearson New Zealand Ltd) • Penguin Books (South Africa) (Pty) Ltd,
24 Sturdee Avenue, Rosebank, Johannesburg 2196, South Africa

Penguin Books Ltd, Registered Offices: 80 Strand, London WC2R 0RL, England

Lyrics to "Franklin's Tower" by Robert Hunter, copyright Ice Nine Publishing Company.
Used with permission.

Most Avery books are available at special quantity discounts for bulk purchase for sales promotions, premiums, fund-raising, and
educational needs. Special books or book excerpts also can be created to fit specific needs. For details, write Penguin Group (USA)
Inc. Special Markets, 375 Hudson Street, New York, NY 10014.

Library of Congress Cataloging-in-Publication Data

Burgess, Wes.
The bipolar handbook for children, teens, and families: real-life questions with up-to-date answers/Wes Burgess.
p.   cm.
Includes index.
ISBN 978-1-58333-307-5
1. Manic-depressive illness in children—Handbooks, manuals, etc.   2. Manic-depressive illness in
adolescence—Handbooks, manuals, etc.   I. Title.
RJ506.D4B865   2008   2008006467
618.92'895—dc22

Printed in the United States of America
1   3   5   7   9   10   8   6   4   2

Book design by Amanda Dewey

In another time's forgotten space
Your eyes looked from your mother's face.
Like wildflower seeds on the sand and stone,
May the four winds blow you safely home.

—ROBERT HUNTER

Contents

Introduction

Rebecca is in shock. The doctor has just told her that her daughter, Becky, has bipolar disorder. What is this illness? What can she do about it? How will her family cope? With his busy schedule, the doctor did not have time to sit down and answer her questions. Where can she go for answers?

Tom's daughter Lori is depressed. Sometimes her pain is so great that she does not feel like living. She has been to doctors and therapists who treat depression, but nothing seems to help. Some of the medications even seem to make Lori's depression worse. Tom would do anything for his daughter but he has run out of ideas. What can he do next?

Tracy's young boy Richie cannot be calmed. He is up and down so much that he can't finish his meals. He talks constantly, and he throws a fit if he cannot have his way. The school counselor said Richie had attention deficit hyperactivity disorder (ADHD), but the treatments have only helped a little. Tracy has heard that some hyperactive children have something called bipolar disorder. How can she find out more about this condition?

Sue is sure there is something wrong with her child Bob, but she cannot get any satisfactory explanations for his condition. She consulted a therapist who told her that Bob is just anxious and he will grow out of it. The family doctor mentioned bipolar disorder, but he said he was not sure. How can Sue find out for herself?

Louis is a teen who has recently been treated for bipolar disorder and now is doing much better. However, his parents, brothers, and sisters are exhausted from helping him with his problems and the family is growing apart. How can they find out how to cope with his illness and stay healthy, as a family?

You can find the answers to all these questions and many more in this book.

For the last twenty years, I have written down the most commonly asked questions from bipolar children, their parents, and their families. I have asked other professionals what questions they are asked about childhood bipolar disorder, and I scoured Internet Web sites and chat rooms to find questions that had not been satisfactorily answered by other patients' doctors and therapists. *The Bipolar Handbook for Children, Teens, and Families* contains all of these most-asked questions about bipolar disorder with up-to-date answers. No doubt, you will find answers to *your* questions here.

The Bipolar Handbook for Children, Teens, and Families explains the illness called bipolar disorder, its causes, and how to recognize it. It discusses how to treat the illness with lifestyle changes, medications, therapy, and relaxation training. It addresses the difficulties parents experience making tough decisions that affect their child's health. There are chapters covering the everyday aspects of parenting and success in school, as well as how to prevent and deal with emergencies. An entire chapter is devoted to Internet sources for information, help, and support groups, and there are recommended book lists for parents and for children.

There are more than a million children with bipolar disorder in the United States. Most depression in children in this country is probably caused by bipolar disorder. The bipolar children who are mistakenly being treated for major depression, attention problems, obsessive-compulsive disorder, and autism are getting worse.

I wrote *The Bipolar Handbook for Children, Teens, and Families* to be like a friendly chat with a trusted family physician who knows how to address your own personal worries and fears and who solves problems like yours on a regular basis. I want it to be as if I were sitting down with you and your child face-to-face, so that I can give you individual counsel and cutting-edge information. I want to give you data that have not yet reached textbooks, reference books, or the press, in a form that is easy to understand and to use. Most of all, I really want to stimulate your desire to find out everything there is to know about helping your bipolar child to be healthy and happy. Let's not waste any more time.

THE
BIPOLAR
HANDBOOK
FOR CHILDREN, TEENS, AND FAMILIES

1.

WHAT IS BIPOLAR DISORDER IN CHILDREN?

. . . .

In order to help our children with bipolar disorder, we must become experts on every aspect of the condition and learn every trick in the book. Only then can we be assured that our children will get the treatment, education, and opportunities that they deserve.

Bipolar disorder is a serious disease of the nervous system that affects children and adults. Changes in brain function and an imbalance in brain chemicals causes bipolar disorder, which in turn causes inappropriate emotions, thoughts, and behavior. In children, bipolar disorder is often first noticed when they begin to have poor school performance, poor attention, depression, or behavior problems.

What does the term "bipolar disorder" mean?

The term "bipolar disorder" is somewhat of a misnomer, since it refers to an outdated characterization of pure mania alternating with pure depression (manic depression). We now know that bipolar disorder is a condition that affects many mental and physical processes and is much more than highs or lows. In addition to changes in happiness and sadness, bipolar disorder can produce emotions of anger, anxiety, avoidance, boldness, bravery, ecstasy, fear, idealization, irritability, jealousy, panic, resentment, and shyness in your child. Bipolar disorder can make it hard for your child to get to sleep, wake up, eat normally, and maintain normal body weight. Poor judgment, impulsivity, obsessive thoughts and behaviors, procrastination, and poor motivation affect your child's ability to learn and go to school. One of the most important problems your bipolar child faces is an increased vulnerability to stress, making it difficult for him or her to get past disappointments, frustrations, self-criticism, uncertainty, and confusion.

Until now, I only heard about bipolar disorder occurring in adults. Is it rare in children?

In 2003, a study by the Child and Adolescent Bipolar Foundation found that 750,000 children had bipolar disorder, beginning at preschool or older. With growing population and improved diagnosis, I estimate there are well over one million children with bipolar disorder in the United States. Through them, bipolar disorder affects the lives of their parents, grandparents, siblings, and friends. Psychiatrists, pediatricians, family doctors, psychotherapists, nurses, and social workers spend a large proportion of their time helping these children and their families reach health and happiness. If we include these people, I estimate that childhood bipolar disorder touches the lives of more than six million people in this country alone.

Studies show that 12 percent of bipolar children begin showing symptoms between five and nine years of age and 30 percent of bipolar cases start before fourteen years of age. Of course, this only includes the children whose bipolar disorder has been identified. More than half of the children suffering from bipolar disorder are misdiagnosed or never diagnosed at all.

Do you see many young children who have bipolar disorder?

Bipolar disorder can first appear in children as early as preschool. The youngest child I have treated with clear bipolar disorder was five years of age. She was manic and showed the same symptoms that you would expect to see in an adult with bipolar mania. The majority of children who are brought to me for depression turn out to have bipolar disorder. Most of these children are misdiagnosed several times before they are brought to my office. Untreated, their symptoms continue until adulthood.

I read that there are more cases of bipolar disorder every year. Is this diagnosis a fad?

We are certainly finding more cases due to improved detection and an increased realization that children can suffer from bipolar disorder. However, many doctors believe that treatment of bipolar depressed children with antidepressants has caused a generation of worsening bipolar disorder in these children, whose bipolar conditions have become more severe and more difficult to treat. Modern doctors are more careful to distinguish bipolar depression from other problems and to treat it with appropriate bipolar medications instead of antidepressants.

I read that bipolar disorder gets worse over time. How can I keep my son from getting worse?

Untreated bipolar disorder usually grows worse with age. However, I think that the progression of the disease can be suspended in your son if he is treated early and appropriately.

Whenever your son has a severe bipolar episode, his brain undergoes changes, particularly in an area called the amygdala, which can pass on these changes to other parts of his brain. The correct medications can stop bipolar episodes from happening, and some bipolar medications can even stimulate your son's brain to grow and repair brain cells. When bipolar episodes are controlled, I believe that worsening of your son's disease will dramatically slow or stop.

How serious is my son's bipolar disorder if it is not brought under control?

Untreated bipolar disorder can interfere with your son's health, family relationships, and school progress. If left untreated, as an adult your son will be twice as likely to be unemployed and three times more likely to be divorced than his schoolmates.

Is bipolar disorder associated with any general medical illness?

Migraine headaches, heart disease, obesity, and diabetes are more common in bipolar individuals than the rest of the population. In my experience, children with bipolar disorder also have more asthma, eczema, psoriasis, and irritable bowel syndrome than other children. This could be linked with poor control of the body chemical adrenaline caused by bipolar disorder.

However, bipolar disorder may protect against some disorders. According to one study, your child may be less susceptible to lymphoma and metastatic cancer than the rest of the population, but I do not know why at this time.

What is the worst thing bipolar disorder could do to my child?

The worst thing bipolar disorder can do to children is to keep them from discovering and using their own special gifts.

WHAT IS BIPOLAR DISORDER?

Bipolar disorder is an illness of the brain and nervous system caused by a change in the biochemistry and connectivity of your child's nervous system. Genetics, brain chemical imbalance, and changes in the signals transmitted in your child's brain interfere with emotions, behavior, and, most important, with the process of thinking.

Did I give my son bipolar disorder by bad parenting?

Absolutely not! Bipolar disorder is not caused by poor parenting or disappointments during childhood. It is not caused by food allergies, sugar, gluten, vitamin insufficiencies, or anything you give to your child. Bipolar disorder is not caused by poverty, deprivation, discrimination, or disenfranchisement. Bipolar illness can be found in every nation and every culture from the beginning of written history. Bipolar symptoms worsen under stressful conditions, but stress did not cause your son's bipolar disorder.

How likely is it that my son inherited X the disorder?

There is a 20 percent chance that your son's bipolar disorder appeared spontaneously and cannot be linked to any family member. However, studies have shown a genetic link to bipolar disorder and your son may have another family member with bipolar disorder within the last two generations. For example, if your son had an identical twin, that twin would have a 70 percent chance of also having bipolar disorder. When both parents are bipolar, there is a 50 percent chance of bipolar disorder in their child. If one parent has the disorder, we estimate their child has about a 20 percent risk.

Scientists believe that some of the DNA that is passed down through families contains genetic material that produces bipolar disorder. Genes that code for bipolar disorder are located on chromosomes 4p, 12q, 18p-q, 22q, and others.

Give me a simple, straightforward explanation of what causes bipolar disorder.

Bipolar disorder is caused by changes in the brain. I like to think of bipolar disorder as a spot in your child's brain where a small number of brain cells are not working the way they should. These bipolar brain cells fire too quickly or too slowly, upsetting the synchrony of other brain cells in their path. If pathways controlling emotion, attention, and thought control pass through this dysfunctional area, the brain cells in these pathways will be disturbed, producing disturbances in emotion, attention, and thought control.

I believe that this small group of dysfunctional bipolar brain cells accounts for all bipolar symptoms, including bipolar depression, bipolar mania, and bipolar mixed symptoms, as well as the anger, anxiety, distractibility, fear, panic, poor focus, underperformance in school, and behavior problems that often come from bipolar disorder.

Where are the dysfunctional bipolar brain cells located in the brain?

We know of several interconnected brain areas associated with bipolar disorder. One is called the temporal area, located under your temples. Injuries and epilepsy in the temporal area produce symptoms like mania and bipolar depression. The mood stabilizer medications that are used to treat bipolar disorder also treat temporal area disorders, such as epilepsy. I have tested many bipolar children who had cognitive problems associated with the temporal area.

So how does this explain how bipolar treatment works in my son?

Mood stabilizer medications make your son's bipolar brain cells fire normally. With mood stabilizer medications, we can make these bipolar brain cells fire the way they were supposed to, neither too slowly nor too fast. Then the pathways crossing through the area of these brain cells will also behave normally. So, when these bipolar brain cells are functioning normally, your son's bipolar symptoms improve and he can function normally and use his special talents and abilities to their fullest.

Is it all really that simple?

No, it never is. The real situation is more complicated. For example, the brain pathways involved in bipolar disorder are connected and pass through many areas of the brain where they are affected by numerous brain chemicals. Different experiences contribute to different habits in different children. However, in my opinion, following this simple model will help your son get successful treatment of his bipolar disorder.

What brain chemicals are out of balance in my bipolar daughter?

Brain cells located in areas called the hypothalamus and pituitary areas (closely connected with the temporal area) control an important brain chemical called adrenaline. The body releases adrenaline in large quantities in response to stress. If cells in these areas are dysfunctional, then adrenaline production can be too high or too low. If there were too much adrenaline in the body, you would see sped-up, manic symptoms such as agitation, anxiety, distractibility, hyperactivity, insomnia, irritability, and poor attention. If adrenaline levels were too low, you would notice slowed-down, bipolar depressive symptoms like fatigue, difficulty starting and finishing projects, low motivation, oversleeping, and weight gain. This is called the adrenaline theory of bipolar disorder. (Note that we shall call this important brain chemical by its well-known name of adrenaline, although the scientifically correct names are epinephrine in the body and norepinephrine in the brain.)

In addition to adrenaline, we know that the brain chemicals serotonin, dopamine, glutamate, and glycine can also have an effect on bipolar symptoms, often to worsen them.

Are there hormones that are imbalanced in my bipolar grandson's nervous system?

The cells in the areas of your grandson's brain that control adrenaline (the hypothalamus and pituitary areas) also trigger the release of steroid hormones when your grandson is under stress. These steroid stress hormones can cause changes in your grandson's emotions, thoughts, and behavior. We can find an example of the effects of elevated stress steroid hormones in bodybuilders who take supplemental steroid hormones during training. In some of these individuals, supplemental steroid hormones cause emotional breakdown and psychosis not unlike severe bipolar disorder. Some research suggests that high levels of these stress steroid hormones may even kill cells in some areas of the brain (the frontal lobes and hippocampus). An imbalance of stress steroid hormones is another contributor to bipolar illness.

What is the main contribution of environment and experience to bipolar disorder?

Many bipolar children are quite vulnerable to stress, and extreme stressors, traumatic experiences, or unhealthy environments can make it harder for these children to function in their daily lives. Moreover, starting early in childhood, children with untreated bipolar disorder develop coping strategies to try to deal with their disorder. These can include avoidance, procrastination, denial, inflexibility, or anger episodes. Once bipolar disorder is treated, however, these coping strategies are no longer needed and psychotherapy can help children minimize them or drop them altogether. As a child grows older, bad habits of thought and behavior become harder to reverse, so it pays to begin treatment early.

Can you give me an example of a bad habit or problem-coping strategy that a bipolar child might learn?

I was recently speaking with a teenaged patient who had been troubled all her life with bipolar irritability and anger, and she had developed angry habits. Even after we had brought her irritability under control with appropriate treatment, she continued to have trouble interacting with other people. One day she came in and told me that she had had a great revelation.

"I realized that even though someone frustrates me, I don't have to get angry at them," she said. "I can ignore them or say something clever or just leave or do anything I want!" This girl had been getting angry at other people for such a long time that it had never occurred to her that she did not *have* to become angry when things did not go her way.

"It always seemed like the only thing to do," she said. "Now I realize that I have many choices of how to handle frustrating situations." After bipolar symptoms are diminished, you can help your child drop unnecessary habits like these.

BIPOLAR CHILDREN AND OUR CULTURE

When your child's bipolar disorder is successfully treated, he or she will look and act like everyone else. However, the media portray people with bipolar disorder as if they were wild and out of control. In this way, they worsen the public stigma against bipolar children.

Unfortunately, many people base their understanding of bipolar disorder on lurid portrayals of psychotic bipolar individuals on television, in movies, and in the press. For example, one television movie portrayed a bipolar man huddling naked in his neighbor's garden, out of his mind. Another media portrayal showed a man looking at the sky and laughing wildly as he walked out on the open girders of a skyscraper. It is ironic that the entertainment industry stereotypes bipolar disorder in this way, given that there are people in the entertainment industry who have bipolar disorder and lead normal, successful lives.

What is bipolar stigma? How does it affect my daughter?

Stigma is ignorance and discrimination against your daughter and anyone else with bipolar disorder. Bipolar stigma is apparent when you tell your friends about your daughter's condition and you see their faces fall. Bipolar stigma is apparent when your daughter is treated differently at school and in other activities because she is bipolar.

What is the worst effect of bipolar stigma on my son?

Stigma is worst when it makes your son feel embarrassed about himself. If your son had a leg or arm injury then he would have no need for embarrassment, because his difficulty would be obvious and easily comprehended. However, your son has nothing that can be bandaged and easily understood by others. In addition, bipolar disorder may make your son quite concerned about what others think about him, and this worsens the feeling of stigmatization. The fact is, when your son's bipolar disorder is successfully treated, he will feel and act like any other child.

What is the worst public misconception about bipolar disorder in children?

The worst notion about any child nowadays is that he or she will go out of control. The public, which has no idea of the official bipolar diagnostic criteria, follows the media's interpretation that people suffering from bipolar disorder experience complete loss of control and exhibit unpredictable, "crazy" behavior. It does not help when bipolar television and movie stars act up inappropriately to get publicity and notoriety.

A health professional told me my son couldn't be bipolar because he doesn't act "crazy."

Unfortunately, this person may have been trying to reassure you. Unless they were trained in psychiatry, many health professionals' only contact with bipolar disorder was with the severe, hospitalized cases they saw early in their training, and your son certainly does not look anything like them. Nevertheless, pretending nothing is wrong will not help your son get the help he needs, either.

Why don't doctors and therapists want to talk about my daughter having bipolar disorder?

Your child's caretakers may hesitate to give your daughter a bipolar diagnosis for fear of being wrong and causing her to be stigmatized. However, refusing to diagnose your daughter can delay her treatment and deprive her of months or years of healthy functioning.

In addition, I think that doctors, therapists, counselors, and teachers sometimes feel threatened when they are dealing with bipolar disorder. When they see an intelligent, talented, lovable girl who has bipolar disorder they may realize how easily this illness could have found them instead. They can easily imagine their own beloved children falling prey to what seems a daunting disease, and their personal fears may affect their outlook.

Why are other parents so uncomfortable hearing about my son's bipolar disorder?

They do not want to imagine that their own children might also suffer from a problem like bipolar disorder. It is easier to ignore, deny, discount, deride, or discriminate against life's problems than to face them. It is a strategy that many people use, but there is no place for it in caring for your son's bipolar disorder.

What do other children think of my child?

Schoolmates often find their bipolar friends exciting because their attitude and behavior seem so different. Bullies and antisocial schoolmates like bipolar children who can be manipulated into breaking the rules, acting impulsively, and being the scapegoat for their inappropriate or illegal behavior. Mean-spirited children will use every opportunity to take out their anger and insecurity on any child who seems a little different.

Does our culture value bipolar attributes?

For all of the stigma against bipolar disorder, it is amazing how much our culture idolizes bipolar symptoms. Moodiness and sensitivity are admired in young television and film stars like James Dean. Our culture adulates manic symptoms in characters like James Bond who work through the night, never seem to tire, demonstrate irritability and aggressivity, develop dramatic personal relationships, and have a high sexual drive. Just turn on the television and you will see these symptoms portrayed as exciting and attractive. This ambiguity just makes it harder for bipolar children to get their symptoms under control. Our culture offers little help for children suffering from bipolar disorder.

Do you think that our economy exploits children with bipolar disorder?

Our economy certainly benefits from bipolar disorder. Bipolar children often believe the unrealistic claims of health faddists and want to buy worthless products advertised on television and in teen magazines. Bipolar children's wish for others to like them helps drive the childhood fashion industry. The bipolar child's need to have the best of everything inflates his or her parents' spending.

I hate the stigma my bipolar son faces every day. How can we get rid of stigma?

Stigma draws its power from ignorance and fear. Use your influence in person or on the Internet to correct other people's misconceptions. This book is one attempt to penetrate this ignorance and fear by telling the bipolar story the way it is.

HOPE FOR BIPOLAR CHILDREN

Sometimes we are so overwhelmed with our bipolar children's problems that we forget about the attributes that make them special. In my experience, bipolar children are more likely to possess creativity and intelligence, as well as artistic, design, and musical talent. There have been many presidents, kings, generals, heroes, famous musicians, writers, composers, painters, actors, film directors, and religious leaders who were bipolar. Now that bipolar disorder is losing its stigma, celebrities, politicians, music stars, and other respected individuals are revealing that they have the disease. Most of these individuals' symptoms have been controlled for years with the right medical treatment.

Can I be hopeful about my daughter's future?

Absolutely! When her bipolar disorder is successfully treated, your daughter should have a happy and successful life. Sixty percent of bipolar children go on to college. Bipolar children are often drawn to the entertainment business, where their special outlook, creativity, and sensitivity help them to be successful writers, designers, actors, producers, and directors.

What can I do to help other children with bipolar disorder?

Speak out, connect with other parents of bipolar children, join local and online support groups, and share your knowledge and experiences with other parents of bipolar children. In the process, you will get some helpful ideas in return. Join and become an officer in bipolar organizations at the local, national, and international levels. Write, spread the word, and push for public awareness of the truth about bipolar disorder. Join lobbying movements to make our leaders aware of what we want for our bipolar children. The resources in Chapter 12 will give you some places to start.

2.

MAKE SURE YOUR CHILD GETS THE CORRECT DIAGNOSIS

. . . .

Traditionally, we divide bipolar symptoms into depression and mania, although most children show a mixture of the two. Unfortunately, bipolar disorder is frequently missed or misdiagnosed in children. If we could look inside children's heads and see where the problem was, we could diagnose childhood bipolar disorder correctly 100 percent of the time. However, until we can do this, a lot of time and effort must be expended to make sure bipolar children get the right diagnosis.

Why are you so concerned about diagnosis?

The reason to ensure that your child gets the correct diagnosis is so that he or she can get the right kind of treatment and avoid treatment that could be harmful. The diagnosis tells the doctor where the problem is in the nervous system, which pathways and brain chemicals are located there, and how we can get them to work the way they are supposed to. With this information, the doctor can then offer you a choice of treatments that will work for your child.

Is a diagnosis of bipolar disorder a medical diagnosis or just a description of how someone feels?

Bipolar disorder is a medical condition. As a medical condition, bipolar disorder arises from specific anomalies in the brain and brain chemicals. By comparison, if we say someone is anxious, we are just describing a general reaction that has no specific location in the brain. Anxiety is just a symptom, not a medical condition. Feelings of anxiety can result from many kinds of physiological, psychological, social, and cultural reactions. For example, feelings of anxiety could be a sign of panic disorder or social anxiety disorder, but they could also be a normal reaction to a tense situation.

Bipolar disorder arises from inside our bodies; it changes over time but is always a part of us. By contrast, if we say someone is disappointed and feels low, this is just a temporary reaction to the environment around them and not a medical condition.

The process of diagnosis is an attempt to find out whether the medical condition of bipolar disorder is present or not.

Isn't bipolar disorder different in every child? How can you make generalizations?

There is no doubt that every child is different. All you have to do is to go to a park or playground and you will see that this is true. However, because bipolar disorder is caused by specific brain cells and brain chemicals, the disease itself is remarkably similar from child to child. I like to think of it like this: if you gave a big birthday party and invited only bipolar children, you could walk through the party and see a bunch of kids who were all different. However, if you listened to the children talking or watched their behavior, you would find that they each exhibited symptoms of their bipolar disorder that were, in fact, quite similar. If you talked with the parents of the bipolar children, you would find that they faced the same parenting challenges that you face with your child. So while the children are indeed different, the disease is the same.

How can I face the possibility that something could be wrong with my daughter?

It may not be as bad as you think. Knowing that bipolar disorder is present gives us the opportunity to treat it and to allow your child to be happy and lead a normal life. Bipolar disorder is very treatable and does not cause crippling or death like other chronic diseases from which children suffer, including cancer, cystic fibrosis, epilepsy, polio, and birth defects. I see the diagnosis of bipolar disorder as an opportunity for your child to have the happiness she deserves and to be the person she was meant to be.

Remember, the process of finding out about your daughter does not create problems. However, if we find out what the problems *are,* we can then start to help her solve them.

Are bipolar depression and mania different disorders?

Mania and bipolar depression are symptoms of the same disorder. The same dysfunctional bipolar brain cells cause both bipolar depression and mania symptoms, and both types of symptoms resolve with bipolar treatment.

I'm not a doctor. How can I be better equipped to help with the diagnosis of my child?

You cannot always count on the professionals who care for your child to be familiar with bipolar disorder or its diagnosis. This is why you'll find the official diagnostic criteria for bipolar disorder on pages 265–266.

I don't think my grade-schooler has bipolar
    disorder. He matches the criteria, but
    there is a good cause for every symptom.

There is usually a good cause for bipolar symptoms. Bipolar disorder is a
stress-related condition, and stressful life events usually precede bipolar symptoms. However, even if there are good causes for your son's condition, it
does not mean that he should suffer needlessly when treatment can alleviate his painful symptoms.

SYMPTOMS OF BIPOLAR DEPRESSION

Symptoms caused by bipolar disorder were identified as early as 1000
B.C. by a Turkish doctor named Aretaeus. By 1875, "manic depressive" disorder was recognized as a distinct illness by European doctors. Dr. Emil
Leonhard followed by clarifying the difference between bipolar depression
and unipolar major depression in the 1950s. Unipolar major depression is a
different disorder located in a different part of the brain and associated with
different brain chemicals than bipolar depression.

Is bipolar disorder in children mainly
    depression or mainly mania?

Childhood bipolar disorder is mainly about depression. Studies show that,
over their lifetime, children with bipolar disorder experience depression three
times more often than mania. Moreover, many experts now think that most
depression in children is caused by bipolar disorder.

What would I see in my son that would
    indicate bipolar depression?

You know it is depression when your son does not enjoy his usual activities and avoids doing pleasant, enjoyable activities. Your son may be overly

pessimistic, obsessed with negative thoughts, and unable to imagine that things could ever get better. He may think of himself as undesirable, fat, ugly, incapable, a failure, an impostor, or a fake. Thoughts of suicide may be present, often precipitated by disappointing or irritating events.

What emotions does my son feel when he's depressed?

Your bipolar depressed son can feel negative emotions like sadness, anger, anxiety, boredom, emptiness, hopelessness, irritability, loneliness, and panic at the same time, as if they were one big emotion. He may have some difficulty distinguishing types of emotions, and he may simply label all his bad feelings depression, panic, or anxiety.

What physical feelings does my girl experience because of bipolar depression?

Your bipolar depressed daughter may report that she is tired, doesn't want to do anything, or wants to sleep all day. She thinks she will accomplish a task but then, when she looks up, the evening is gone, and it is time for her to go to bed.

Many bipolar depressed children feel a peculiar physical feeling they describe as "not feeling like me," "feeling like something's wrong," or feeling "not right in my body." These feelings resemble jet lag in adults, and may come from their bodies' inability to keep up with the changing seasons and day lengths throughout the year.

An Official Diagnosis of Atypical/Bipolar Depression

I believe that bipolar depression is so distinctive that it usually can be differentiated from other types of depression by direct examination, supplemented by information from parents and family. However, many doctors will not give the diagnosis of bipolar depression unless they find evidence of a prior manic episode. A few doctors still believe that bipolar depression is the same as unipolar major depression.

How would bipolar depression be diagnosed in my son?

At the present time, there is no listing for "bipolar depression" in the official manual of medical diagnoses. "Physical slowing with or without over-sleeping" is the way one major authority characterizes bipolar depression (see *Kaplan & Sadock's Comprehensive Textbook of Psychiatry,* Chapter 12).

From my years of observing and treating bipolar patients, I believe that the diagnosis psychiatrists know as "atypical depression" is most like bipolar depression, and several studies support this similarity. However, not all professionals agree. You can find the official definition of atypical depression in the *American Psychiatric Association's Diagnostic and Statistical Manual, Volume IV, Text Revision (DSM-IV-TR),* reproduced in Appendix 1. I have adapted this definition of atypical (bipolar) depression for my patients as follows. Remember that bipolar disorder is a disorder of the brain; these feelings, experiences, and behaviors are just visible signs of bipolar depression that we use for diagnosis.

The Criteria Used to Diagnose Atypical Depression (Bipolar Depression)
Conditions A, B, C, and D must be satisfied.

☐ A. Your child's mood is depressed most of the day for two weeks or more.
  OR
  Your child has lost interest in activities that used to give him or her pleasure.
☐ B. Even when your child is depressed, his or her mood may brighten for a short time.
  AND
C. At least two of the following:
  ☐ Your child has increased appetite or significant weight gain.
  ☐ Your child tries to sleep too much and has difficulty getting up in the morning.
  ☐ Your child experiences significant physical fatigue, which may result in low motivation.
  ☐ Your child has a long-standing pattern of easily hurt feelings.
☐ D. These symptoms cause problems in major areas of life (like school, family, or friendships).

Other features that I often see in bipolar depression include anxiety, distractibility, inability to finish projects, intrusive thoughts, memory problems, poor self-care, procrastination, and social withdrawal.

Why do you adopt the criteria of atypical depression for bipolar depression?

When my bipolar patients are depressed, they describe the symptoms now called atypical depression, including oversleeping, weight gain, and physical fatigue with low motivation. Their mood can improve with good news, if only shortly, and they have a lifetime history of easily hurt feelings. Statistically, studies of atypical depression also demonstrate a similarity with bipolar disorder, including onset at an early age, greater prevalence in girls, increased suicidality, and significant interference with life activities. As with other phases of bipolar disorder, atypical depression carries a high risk for substance abuse, panic episodes, and social withdrawal.

How can we improve the accuracy of my son's bipolar depression diagnosis?

Finding other bipolar features can improve the accuracy of the diagnosis. For example, if your depressed son has a relative with bipolar disorder, exhibits activated or manic symptoms, stays up late at night, or exhibits other bipolar features you will find out about in this book, this increases the likeliness that his depression is bipolar depression.

My doctor said that my boy couldn't have bipolar depression unless he has had a manic episode. Until then, the doctor says he will be treated as if he has unipolar major depression.

One study showed that 20 percent of people suffering from bipolar depression have their first manic episode more than six years after their depression starts. This is clearly too long to delay treatment for your son's benefit. More-over, many children with bipolar disorder have mixed symptoms or may never show manic symptoms at all. The key to success in treating childhood bipolar depression is identifying the condition early and starting appropriate treatment for bipolar disorder.

If my preteen daughter doesn't get what she wants, she gets upset like a three-year-old. Why?

Irritability, easily hurt feelings, and immature emotional reactions are important components of bipolar depression. Your daughter may become upset and overreact if she is refused something she wants, has to make sudden decisions, is given foods she does not like, or sees others handling her personal possessions. This emotional immaturity usually goes away with adequate treatment.

Why does my bipolar son do things that get him in trouble and cause him embarrassment?

Bipolar depressed children often show poor judgment. Your son's bipolar disorder makes it hard for him to learn from his past mistakes and causes him difficulty in planning for the future. He may have trouble recognizing when he is doing something that is going to get him into trouble.

Why is my bipolar depressed child so persnickety?

Because of the physiological changes produced by bipolar disorder (see Chapter 1), children with bipolar depression are often more sensitive to stimuli than others. They often feel discomfort from bright lights, loud noises, cold temperatures, or too many things going on at once. Children may appear sensitive to changing seasons, and bipolar problems often increase around the end of winter and the end of summer (when day length and daylight saving time change).

What is wrong with my bipolar son's sleep?

Bipolar depression can make it difficult for your son to get out of bed in the morning, and he may want to stay in bed or on the couch for hours. Your son may complain of sleepiness, fatigue, and feeling slowed down during the day. Although bipolar depressed children may feel sleepy during the day, they often have difficulty getting to bed, and may try to stay up late at night.

My bipolar depressed son cannot seem to get going. Do other parents see this?

Bipolar depression may interfere with your son's ability to wake up and get ready for his day. He may develop poor hygiene habits that interfere with brushing his teeth regularly, taking showers, or putting on clean clothes. He may procrastinate or spend minutes or hours daydreaming or staring into space. He may experience problems starting projects and, unless you remind him, he may not start studying, do his homework, do chores, or clean his room.

My bipolar child has no motivation, and the counselor said it's from bad self-image. What do you think?

Irrespective of self-image, bipolar depression makes it physically and mentally difficult for your son to initiate and finish projects. Bipolar depressed children often develop habits of extreme procrastination, relying on the energy of potential failure to get their projects done at the last minute. Part of this is a physical effect of bipolar depression combined with the extra difficulty bipolar children have with some school subjects, especially mathematics. Bipolar depressed children complain that they cannot focus and their bodies feel like lead.

By the way, just because he can concentrate for hours on tasks where he excels (like playing electronic games) does not mean he is being lazy with his homework. The high stimulation, artistic graphics, music, and nonlinear play of video games appeal to the special strengths that many children with bipolar disorder possess.

My depressed daughter seems terribly shy. Do other bipolar depressed children show this?

In severe bipolar depression, children hole up in their rooms, refuse to return or initiate telephone calls, ignore or break up with their friends, stop talking with their families, and show an unwillingness to participate in social, community, or family functions. If this is happening to your daughter, it will probably get better with appropriate bipolar treatment.

Do bipolar depressed children tend to be overweight? My child has steadily gained weight over the past few months.

Bipolar depressed children can gain weight prodigiously. Bipolar depression may make your child crave chocolate or starches, or trigger binge eating. The daytime fatigue of bipolar depression may cause him or her to spend a lot of time sitting and lying down. This is a prescription for weight gain. Although you may meet with resistance from your child, my suggestion is to increase exercise, eliminate chocolate, and cut down on starches.

Q My bipolar depressed girl has always had
sudden, extreme mood swings to rage
or tears, at the slightest provocation.
Is this common?

Yes. It is common for bipolar children's emotions to flip-flop into extreme emotions and stay there for minutes or hours. Bipolar depression can cause your child to suddenly scream, rage out of control, or cry inconsolably.

EVEN CASUAL REMARKS CAN SEEM HURTFUL TO BIPOLAR DEPRESSED CHILDREN

• • • • • •

When a child suffers from bipolar depression, a simple "Good morning" can elicit hurt or anger. Bipolar depression can cause your child to find slights, innuendos, and unpleasant implications in the mildest things you say and do.

You: "Good morning!"
BP Child: "What's so good about it?"
          "It may seem good to you but what about me?"
          "Are you trying to torture me by pointing out how you feel good and I feel bad?"
You: "Congratulations! You earned a B on your math test!"
BP Child: "Don't congratulate me. It was an easy test."
          "That just shows how inferior I am to the kids who did better than me."
          "Are you trying to make me miserable? You always say I should make As."
You: "You look nice today."
BP Child: "You have to say that. You're my mother."
          "If I look so nice, why don't I have any friends?"
          "Are you making fun of me?"

Remember that it is not *what* you say that is the problem. Your son's bipolar depression is the problem. Better treatment of the illness will help solve this problem.

How can I keep from hurting my son's
feelings? No matter what I say, he
finds something hurtful in it.

The tendency to get upset easily is usually present in the background even
before clear bipolar depressed symptoms develop. Easily hurt feelings will
get better with treatment of bipolar disorder.

BIPOLAR MANIA

The Greeks and Romans first used the term mania to describe people
who were agitated and euphoric. Nowadays, mania refers to the mental, emotional, and physical experiences that comprise the activated stage of bipolar disorder. These symptoms are called manic symptoms, and when they
predominate, the condition is called a manic episode.

My son looks irritable and angry, not
euphoric. Could he still have
bipolar mania?

The irritability and anger your son feels are key features of bipolar mania.
Doctors are taught to expect euphoria or feeling high in mania, but irritability alone is sufficient to diagnose bipolar mania. Irritability and anxiety are
much more common than euphoria in bipolar manic children. Some doctors think that bipolar children are angrier than bipolar adults, but I think
there is plenty of anger to go around for everyone.

What do doctors look for to diagnose
bipolar mania?

There are specific official criteria published by the American Psychiatric Association for doctors to use to diagnose bipolar mania in children and adults.

Remember that bipolar disorder is a disorder of the brain; these are just the behaviors and experiences that we can see and use to detect bipolar mania.

The Criteria Doctors Use to Diagnose Bipolar Mania

You can find the official definition of bipolar mania in the *American Psychiatric Association's Diagnostic and Statistical Manual, Vol. IV, Text Revision (DSM-IV-TR),* reproduced in Appendix 1. I have adapted this definition for my patients as follows:

Conditions A, B, and C must be satisfied.

- ☐ A. Your child shows a persistently irritable, expansive, or elevated mood lasting a week or more.
  AND
- B. At least three or four of the following (four if your child's mood is only irritable):
  - ☐ Your child has nighttime insomnia or may feel rested after only a few hours of sleep.
  - ☐ Your child is very talkative and often interrupts others' speech or cannot stop talking.
  - ☐ Your child's thoughts move rapidly and it may feel like his or her mind is racing.
  - ☐ Your child is easily distractible and his or her thoughts and speech go off track easily.
  - ☐ Your child is overfocused on school, social, or sexual activities, and/or feels agitated or edgy.
  - ☐ Your child makes impulsive decisions that may result in harm or punishment.
  - ☐ Your child has an exaggerated idea of his or her own importance, power, or need to be served (for example, always having to be right, trying to control or bully family and friends, or talking back and fighting with adults in authority even when they are in the wrong).
- ☐ C. These symptoms cause problems in major areas of life (like school, family, or friendships).

It is very important to note that the dominant emotion in mania is often irritability and anger. Many professionals misdiagnose mania because they think that your child's mood must be elated and euphoric. To have mania you do not need to be smiling, laughing, happy, high, or elated, or show any other elevated emotion. The most common symptoms that I see in my patients are angry mood, rapid speech, distractibility, and sleeping problems.

The National Institutes of Mental Health publishes a list of manic symptoms that you may read in Appendix 2.

How is bipolar disorder diagnosed differently in children and in adults?

The official diagnostic criteria are the same for both children and adults. Although separate child criteria and tests have been suggested, in my experience the same diagnostic criteria diagnose manic episodes just as well in both children and adults.

My daughter has bipolar mania and she is always on the go. Is this common?

At home, manic children are often overactive and always in motion, and cannot sit down or stick to one activity for more than a few minutes. Your daughter may start projects that are never finished and try to do several tasks at once without being successful at any of them. Your daughter may feel bored and may want stimulation and activity every minute, even if it elicits discomfort or unpleasant reactions from the others around her.

Why can't my bipolar manic son sleep?

Because of bipolar mania, your son's body and thoughts may be too active to sleep. Your son may stay up all night, get up early in the morning, and be overly energetic all day long. Even as he begins to become physically fatigued, he may fight falling asleep as long as possible. Eventually, this ends in physical and mental exhaustion and he may sleep heavily for a day or more. Unfortunately, when he has recharged his batteries, he may return to his frenetic activity.

Q My bipolar boy never seems to think before
      he acts.

Bipolar mania can make your son act impulsively without thinking things
through first. His impulsive speech may get him into trouble in the classroom for speaking out of turn and interrupting his teacher. He may appear
blunt or uncaring when he says the first thing that comes into his mind.

Q What is going on when my bipolar manic
      kid talks? He seems to be speaking a
      mile a minute.

Bipolar manic children often talk too fast, too loudly, and too much. Your
son may speak so rapidly that it is hard for anyone else to get a word in edge-
wise. In fact, he may speak so fast that he veers off topic and goes off on
tangents. In an attempt to get his ideas out before distraction knocks them
out of his head, your son may interrupt others, answer for them, and try to
finish their sentences.

    Needless to say, this can make other people feel left out and less inter-
ested in talking to your son in the future.

Q My boy's emotions seem precarious. They
      can change in an instant when he's manic.

As in depression, your bipolar son's manic emotions can change rapidly at the
slightest hint of perceived insult or embarrassment. However, instead of causing inconsolable sadness, mania may suddenly cause him to become irritable,
angry, belligerent, or raging. Often the sequence is indignation, anger, rage,
and then sadness and embarrassment. Doctors and the public are most familiar with the overly optimistic, elated, high manic mood, but overall, anger
is the emotion I see most often in bipolar mania.

On Sunday, we went to my sister's funeral and my bipolar son kept laughing. Why?

Sometimes bipolar mania causes children to break out in inexplicable grins, fits of giggles, or laughter that they cannot explain and that can be annoying or disconcerting to others. Help your son become more aware of his facial expressions by gently describing how he looks. Then he can try to match his facial expression to the situation.

Our family doesn't like our bipolar manic son's attitude. He's prideful and too full of himself.

In children, bipolar mania often produces a markedly narcissistic opinion of oneself. Bipolar mania can cause your son to imagine that he is extremely powerful, unusually handsome, brilliant, invincible, and omnipotent. He may argue any little point as if he were an expert and, no matter what the topic, he may insist that he is always right. Bipolar mania can make your child feel that he always has to win the game and be the center of attention.

What is this thing called hypersociality? I'm worried my bipolar daughter may have it.

Bipolar mania may cause your daughter to be overly outgoing, spend too much time socializing, and act like she is onstage with clever speeches or comedy routines. She may approach strangers as if they are friends, talk to people in public places, and put herself at risk in dangerous social situations. Just as hypersociality is seen in bipolar mania, social avoidance is frequently seen in bipolar depression, and both can be seen when manic and depressed symptoms are mixed.

Why is my bipolar manic daughter so messy?

As a result of poorly organized thoughts, your bipolar manic girl's life and possessions are likely to be in a mess. Your daughter may have a messy room, messy closet, messy backpack, and messy handwriting. Manic children lead a cluttered life, thus the phrase "messy manic."

My daughter seems to be maturing too early. She's already talking about boys.

Unhappily for us adults, bipolar mania can produce an abnormal increase in sexual drive, even in young children. Coupled with impulsivity and an inability to think before acting, your daughter can end up in distracting, destructive relations with girlfriends and boyfriends. You need to be on the lookout for "friends" who may try to take advantage of your girl's sexuality. Inappropriate sexual behavior can ruin reputations, and possessing an increased sexual drive without the maturity to make safe and responsible decisions can result in sexually transmitted diseases and unwanted pregnancies.

What about hypomania? Is my daughter hypomanic?

Officially, children can be called hypomanic when they show the characteristics of mania but their symptoms are brief and do not interfere with normal life activity. However, I seldom see anyone with bipolar manic symptoms that do not interfere significantly with their school, family, and/or social activities. Nevertheless, I know some professionals who prefer the term hypomania because they think that it sounds less threatening and final than mania.

BIPOLAR CYCLING

Bipolar cycling is a clear switch, over the course of the year, between bipolar manic, bipolar depressed, and/or normal states. In adult-onset bipolar disorder, the cycles start once every year or every other year and usually increase to two or more cycles a year. When there are few cycles per year, they often take place in late winter and late summer. Many doctors think that cycles are caused by changes in day length throughout the year, which interferes with the body's biological rhythms.

Why is it helpful for my bipolar child to find out if his illness has a cycle?

It is reassuring when you can begin to see when bipolar disorder is having an influence on your child. Moreover, it can really help your bipolar son to stay well and help you and your family cope with his bipolar disorder if you can predict the changes in his illness. For example, if we knew that Tom would start sleeping late next week, we could prepare ourselves by having him go to bed early and being ready to roust him out of bed in the morning. If we knew that Sally was going to have angry tantrums next week, we could make an extra visit to her doctor and therapist to head this off before it became a problem.

Why are some patterns of bipolar disorder called Type I, Type II, or Type III?

Type I is used to signify classic bipolar disorder with pure bipolar depressed and bipolar manic cycles during the course of the year. Type II is used to designate individuals who mostly show depressed symptoms through the year with just one or more brief manic or hypomanic cycles. It has been suggested that Type II is more responsive to anticonvulsant mood stabilizers (see Chapter 5). Type III has been used to indicate individuals whose bipolar manic symptoms were first awakened by an antidepressant.

My daughter doesn't alternate between depression and mania. Could she still have a cycle?

In my experience, most children with bipolar disorder do not show clear cycles between depression and mania. However, your daughter's symptoms could grow worse at some times of the year and get better during other seasons.

It's been two months since my son had a bipolar episode. Is he okay now?

No. Although your son may not exhibit symptoms now, he may just be in the middle of a cycle. He may appear fine between episodes, but his bipolar disorder is still active, and closer inspection will usually reveal residual bipolar symptoms such as distractibility and poor problem-solving ability.

The therapist said that Ruthie had "rapid cycling." What is that?

Used correctly, the term "rapid cycling" refers to people who show more than two cycles per year. Classic cycles are usually a month or more of pure bipolar depressed or bipolar manic symptoms. However, this term has begun to be used incorrectly to refer to an individual who exhibits extreme emotional changes during the course of a day, usually from calm to angry, happy to sad, or quiet to excited for minutes or hours. We expect that your bipolar daughter will show such daily mood swings and they are not a special condition that needs special treatment. I simply call them "daily mood swings." Moreover, daily mood swings are not part of the official diagnosis of bipolar disorder and do not prove or disprove the existence of bipolar disorder. Extreme daily mood swings are seen in borderline personality disorder, narcissistic personality disorder, impulse-control disorders, intermittent explosive disorder, and other conditions unrelated to bipolar disorder that require different kinds of treatment.

How in the world can we predict what our bipolar twins will do next month?

We can find out if your twins cycle and what these cycles represent by using a Life Events Table (see page 34). First, carefully remove the Life Events Table from the book and make several copies. Then get together with your spouse, children, and other close family members and plot all the important changes in each of your bipolar twins' lives as far back as you can remember. Mark problem months with *D* for depression, *M* for mania, *X* for mixed depressed and manic symptoms, and *Z* for other problems. When the chart is filled out, inspect it, and see if you can find any yearly patterns. See if depression or mania becomes problematic in the same months each year. See if apparently unrelated outside events coincide with or precede bipolar episodes. If there is a pattern, then you can use it to be prepared for problem times and try to head them off in advance.

How useful is the Life Events Table?

It is very useful if you can find patterns in your child's illness. However, it is more useful in older children and adolescents, because young children have not had many years to compare. In addition, the Life Events Table work sheet cannot discriminate between yearly changes due to bipolar disorder and changes due to the school year, holidays, summer activities, and the like. Nevertheless, it will be helpful for your entire family if it can gain a greater understanding of the course of your child's illness.

MIXED BIPOLAR DISORDER

In addition to pure bipolar depression and pure bipolar mania, there is a third kind of bipolar disorder in which depressed and manic states are present at the same time. This condition is called mixed bipolar disorder. One of the pioneers of modern psychiatry, Emile Kraepelin, described mixed bipolar disorder in Europe in 1921. In the last two decades, there has been little interest in mixed bipolar disorder, which was thought to be uncommon. However, recent studies indicate that 40 to 50 percent of bipolar adults

The Life Events Table can be of great help in determining whether your child cycles and when the cycles occur. Fill out this work sheet year by year, charting months when your child had problems or seemed different from usual. Mark *D* in any months when your child was depressed, *M* in any months when your child was manic, and *X* in any month when your child experienced mixed symptoms of depression and mania. Whenever your child had a significant problem with school, family, or friends, mark that month with a *Z,* even if there does not seem to be any connection to bipolar disorder.

The Life Events Table

YEAR	JAN	FEB	MAR	APR	MAY	JUNE	JUL	AUG	SEPT	OCT	NOV	DEC
2015												
2014												
2013												
2012												
2011												
2010												
2009												
2008												
2007												
2006												
2005												
2004												
2003												
2002												
2001												
2000												
1999												
1998												
1997												
1996												
1995												
1994												
1993												
1992												
1991												
1990												
YEAR	JAN	FEB	MAR	APR	MAY	JUNE	JUL	AUG	SEPT	OCT	NOV	DEC

have mixed bipolar disorder, and a majority of bipolar adolescents have the mixed type. In my opinion, most of the bipolar disorder in children and adolescents is mixed bipolar disorder.

Tom seems to have symptoms of bipolar depression and bipolar mania at the same time. When is his cycle?

Children with mixed bipolar disorder usually do not show clear cycles. However, their mixed bipolar symptoms may worsen predictably at certain times of the year. For example, I treated a bipolar adolescent girl who had mixed symptoms all year and did not cycle. However, she usually was depressed in January and, during the last week of June each year, she developed inexplicable rage episodes, screaming and throwing things at her family members. These times were the low and high points of her underlying cycle.

MISDIAGNOSIS

Misdiagnosis is one of the biggest challenges in the treatment of bipolar disorder today. Studies show that bipolar disorder is missed or misdiagnosed about 70 percent of the time. One-quarter of the children suffering from bipolar disorder wait for ten years or more to get the correct diagnosis. Oddly enough, I do not think that bipolar disorder is that difficult for anyone to diagnose, using the official diagnostic criteria. Instead, I think that doctors and other professionals just do not think of the bipolar diagnosis in children and so they do not see it when it is there. By comparison, they expect to see other common conditions like anxiety and attention deficit hyperactivity disorder (ADHD) and so they see those instead.

One study showed that the majority of people who have bipolar disorder were given the wrong diagnosis three or four times before being correctly identified as having bipolar disorder. Of course, if bipolar disorder is not diagnosed, it cannot be treated. If your child is given the wrong diagnosis, he or she will probably get an incorrect treatment that will not help and may hurt.

Unipolar Major Depression

Unipolar major depression is a completely different disease having different symptoms, originating in different locations in the brain, and affecting different brain cells and brain chemicals than bipolar depression. Nevertheless, studies show that 40 percent of bipolar depressed children are initially misdiagnosed with unipolar major depression. Another study showed that more than 50 percent of the children hospitalized for unipolar major depression were eventually found to have bipolar depression instead.

Moreover, these figures only account for the children who finally get the correct diagnosis and do not include all the children who dropped out of sight when their parents found that the treatment for unipolar major depression was not helpful. I think we are grossly underestimating the amount of bipolar disorder in childhood and that as many as 90 percent of clinically depressed children have bipolar depression, not unipolar major depression.

The doctor gave our son a diagnosis of unipolar major depression, not bipolar disorder. How can I be sure the diagnosis is correct?

If your son has bipolar rather than unipolar major depression, his symptoms are more likely to start at an early age. He may have bipolar speech characteristics (e.g., rapid, loud speech, and interrupting others) and racing thoughts. He is likely to be distractible and to have memory problems. Your son may sleep too much or tend to be obsessive when depressed. If a blood relative is bipolar, then a diagnosis of bipolar disorder must be considered.

It is risky to give antidepressants to any depressed child who might have bipolar disorder because they can make his or her condition permanently worse.

Q What problems could result if my daughter is misdiagnosed with unipolar major depression and given antidepressants?

Antidepressants are for treating unipolar major depression, not bipolar depression. Antidepressants work by increasing brain chemicals like adrenaline and dopamine, the very brain chemicals we are trying to get under control in bipolar disorder. Antidepressants can cause children with bipolar depression to become manic, to become more depressed, to become unstable, or to become psychotic. Worse than that, there is good evidence that antidepressants can make your daughter's bipolar disorder permanently worse, with increased symptoms, increased deterioration with age, and decreased ability for bipolar medications to help. There is no reason to risk harming your daughter by giving her antidepressants, because proper bipolar medications (mood stabilizers) treat the source of her bipolar depression by treating the dysfunctional bipolar brain cells that cause bipolar depression.

Attention Deficit Hyperactivity Disorder (ADHD)

A research study showed that 25 percent of the children thought to have ADHD turn out to have bipolar disorder. Technically, a child cannot be given a diagnosis of ADHD if the symptoms are better accounted for by a mood disorder like bipolar disorder.

The reason it is difficult to distinguish ADHD from bipolar disorder is that both disorders interfere with children's attention. In both conditions, children pay poor attention to detail, forget instructions, fail to finish homework, have difficulty with organization, and lose school assignments and study materials. Both conditions cause children to be hyperactive, fidget, run around, shout loudly, blurt out answers, intrude on others, and have difficulty waiting for their turn.

However, we *can* tell ADHD from bipolar disorder because ADHD will not give your child the other diagnostic bipolar symptoms like rapid, pressured speech, insomnia, or grandiosity. The DSM diagnostic criteria make this quite clear. If your child meets the criteria for bipolar mania (see page 26), and these better account for the symptoms, then he or she has bipolar disorder, not ADHD and not both.

Tell us how we, as parents, can tell the difference between ADHD and bipolar disorder in our son.

If your son has bipolar depression, then he will have lost interest in enjoyable activities. He is likely to be fatigued, gain weight, and oversleep. These are not diagnostic symptoms of ADHD.

If your son has bipolar mania, he could experience episodes of irritability or euphoria. He may be overly talkative, and may have racing thoughts, a fixation on school or personal topics, an inflated sense of self-esteem, high sexual drive, a grandiose sense of importance and power, and an entitled expectation that others should give him whatever he wants. Although these individual symptoms may show up in many children, the overall pattern is characteristic of bipolar disorder, not ADHD.

Children with ADHD do not usually have relatives with bipolar disorder, but the opposite is frequently true. If your son has been given a diagnosis of ADHD and has these bipolar symptoms, he should be evaluated to see if he has bipolar disorder rather than ADHD.

The counselor gave our son tests to diagnose ADHD. Do these test for bipolar disorder too?

Most tests given for ADHD evaluate general components of inattention. They are not designed to determine the presence or absence of bipolar disorder and they do not differentiate bipolar disorder from ADHD. Bipolar disorder causes distractibility that can make your son perform poorly on the tests for ADHD.

Why do we care whether it is ADHD or bipolar disorder? I don't like to label my daughter.

We care about the diagnosis so we can give your daughter the right treatment. Some of the treatments for ADHD such as atomoxetine (Strattera) may permanently worsen your daughter's bipolar disorder. In order to give your daughter the correct treatment, we must know what we are treating. Bipolar disorder and ADHD are located in different parts of the brain, and are associated with different brain cells and different brain chemicals.

Are there any medicines that will treat both ADHD and bipolar disorder?

Clonidine (Catapres) provides some treatment for both (see Chapter 5).

Autistic Spectrum Disorder

If your child is sociable, outgoing, talkative, able to maintain proper social distance, and able to engage in imaginative play, it is unlikely that she or he is autistic. Autistic children usually do not show this pattern of social awareness.

Unfortunately, bipolar depressed children are often withdrawn and difficult for doctors to differentiate from children with autism. The problem comes when the diagnostician places extra weight on the poor formation of peer social relationships. Friendships and social interaction are usually poor in autism, but poor social interactions are also the final common pathway for bipolar depression, unipolar major depression, physical illnesses, poor family health, and many other childhood stresses.

Could my daughter have Asperger's Disorder *and* bipolar disorder?

Lots of children have come to me with a diagnosis of Asperger's Disorder who really had bipolar disorder and responded well to bipolar medicine. I have never seen the two conditions occurring together.

Anxiety Disorders

Most bipolar children feel some symptoms of anxiety such as recurrent, intrusive worried thoughts, and physical symptoms of agitation, edginess, and a sense of "jumping out of their skin." During their lifetimes, 56 percent of bipolar children will experience such severe symptoms that they cause problems with school performance, family life, and/or social relationships. It would be wrong to diagnose their anxiety as a separate *anxiety disorder,* because their anxiety is caused by bipolar disorder and it is relieved by treating the bipolar disorder.

How can I be sure my daughter does not have an anxiety disorder instead of bipolar disorder?

If your daughter suffers from bipolar depression, she will likely feel depressed, want to sleep too much, and experience a paralyzing mental and physical tiredness in addition to anxiety. If your daughter has bipolar mania, she will likely have angry or expansive moods, rapid speech, racing thoughts, poor decision making, obsessive tendencies, and/or an inflated sense of self-esteem in addition to anxiety. If she is bipolar, it is more likely that there is a history of bipolar disorder in the family. None of these bipolar symptoms is part of the diagnostic criteria for anxiety disorders such as panic disorder, generalized anxiety disorder, obsessive-compulsive disorder (OCD), or posttraumatic stress disorder (PTSD). If you were in a room full of children with these disorders, they would not remind you of your daughter.

Why did the emergency room doctor think our son had panic disorder, not bipolar disorder?

If your bipolar son was stressed he may have had symptoms of panic like pounding heart, sweating, shortness of breath, chest pain, nausea, dizziness, chills, hot flushes, numbness, or tingling sensations that could have made the emergency room doctor think of panic disorder. If your bipolar son has an anxiety episode that lasts hours or days, this is probably not a panic attack. Your son's bipolar anxiety will improve when he receives appropriate bipolar medicine. However, the antidepressants and sedatives given to children for panic disorder are not appropriate for your son's bipolar disorder.

My child is shy. Could she have social avoidance disorder or social phobia?

The majority of bipolar children show shyness at some time in their lives. However, if a bipolar child comes to a professional complaining only of severe shyness, the diagnosis of bipolar disorder may be missed.

I heard there is something called generalized anxiety disorder that seems to match my son's symptoms exactly. I went to another doctor and she agreed. Could this be mistaken for bipolar disorder?

Generalized anxiety disorder (GAD) or overanxious disorder of childhood (ODC) is a collection of common anxiety symptoms, including restlessness, edginess, fatigue, problems concentrating, irritability, muscle tension, and sleep disturbance. Every bipolar child I have seen has had one or more of these symptoms. However, GAD does not come with bipolar symptoms or bipolar family history. The official diagnosis of bipolar disorder takes precedence over GAD, so if your son has bipolar symptoms, he probably has bipolar disorder.

I read a book on borderline personality disorder that sounded just like my daughter. Does she have borderline personality disorder instead of bipolar disorder?

Occasionally a bipolar adolescent comes to my office with a diagnosis of borderline personality disorder. The textbook descriptions of patients suffering from borderline personality disorder are somewhat similar to some bipolar individuals, and psychological tests of bipolar individuals sometimes show features of borderline and other personality disorders. A clinician who does not have experience working with many borderline and bipolar patients may find the distinction confusing. Nevertheless, if your daughter meets the diagnostic criteria for bipolar disorder given in Chapter 2, she probably has bipolar disorder, not borderline personality disorder.

Borderline personality disorder is a lifelong condition of unstable relationships, moods, and self-image that includes rapid, short-lasting mood swings to intense sadness, or anxiety, intense displays of anger and rage, and impulsive acts including substance abuse, reckless driving, and sexual indiscretions. Unlike bipolar disorder, borderline personality disorder is also characterized by recurrent suicidality and/or self-injury, extreme reactions to perceived abandonment, and constant feelings of emptiness. Neuropsychological testing shows cognitive deficits in borderline personality disorder that are not shared in bipolar disorder. Moreover, after bipolar children are successfully treated, their psychological testing often shows fewer or no signs of personality disorder remaining.

Overall, I try to reserve the diagnosis of borderline personality disorder for individuals over eighteen years of age who clearly do not have bipolar disorder. If there is any doubt, then a trial of mood stabilizers is indicated before consigning adolescents to a lifetime diagnosis of borderline personality disorder.

Schizophrenia

One of the events that sparked my interest in bipolar disorder was an experience working at a community clinic with an enlightened social worker. Between the two of us, we realized that out of the population of long-diagnosed "schizophrenics" who came to our clinic, most of them really had bipolar disorder that had never been properly treated. When these individuals received the correct medications for bipolar disorder, their lifelong "schizophrenia" disappeared.

Could my daughter's bipolar disorder ever be mistaken for schizophrenia?

If your bipolar daughter is psychotic, she could be misdiagnosed with schizophrenia. This is a problem, because the antipsychotic medicines usually given for schizophrenia may not heal her bipolar disorder. Furthermore, some doctors and therapists have heard that schizophrenic children will never function normally and so they may give up on your daughter's treatment and not push for a full recovery.

My son is hearing voices and thinking that we're all out to get him. Isn't this schizophrenia?

Many doctors automatically think of schizophrenia when they hear about hallucinations or delusional beliefs. However, hallucinations and delusional beliefs are just as common in severe, psychotic bipolar disorder. It is hard to be sure when children are so sick, but I would suspect bipolar disorder if your son talked a lot, told others what to do, had extreme religious beliefs, or was bright, creative, charming, or showy. I would suspect bipolar disorder if he had visual hallucinations or delusions that showed him to be a very important, special person.

What do I do if I think that my daughter's diagnosis is wrong?

The best thing to do is to get a second opinion from a doctor who is a specialist in bipolar disorder. I talk more about that in Chapter 3.

3.

How to Find the
Right Doctor for
Your Child

. . . .

You need a doctor you can trust and work with to get the right treatment for your bipolar child. The ideal relationship is for the three of you to be talking together, learning about bipolar disorder together, and making decisions together.

Ultimately, you must look to your doctor as an educator and resource in your bipolar disorder education. Your doctor must use every available minute to teach you and your child the facts about bipolar disorder. That means that you have to find a doctor who is knowledgeable and is willing to take the time to share his or her knowledge.

Can my pediatrician or primary care physician take good care of my child's bipolar disorder?

You have to find out whether the doctor can or not. Ask about it. If the doctor prefers not to treat bipolar disorder, is not experienced in its treatment, cannot answer your questions, or cannot take the time to develop a dialogue, then you need to find a specialist.

Does my family doctor or pediatrician have training in bipolar disorder?

Although your family doctor or pediatrician received training in psychiatry during medical school, most prefer to leave the complex care of bipolar disorder to the specialists in psychiatry. It is just a matter of numbers. When you have treated thousands of patients with bipolar disorder, you become familiar with the ins and outs of treatment and you figure out what works and what doesn't.

How do I tell my pediatrician I want a psychiatrist to see my bipolar child?

Just ask if he or she can refer you to a psychiatrist. I think that your pediatrician will be happy if you want to call in a specialist. Treatment of bipolar disorder is a challenging task at best.

Who is trained to tell me if my child has bipolar disorder?

I recommend finding a psychiatrist who specializes in bipolar disorder. If one is not available in your area, then check available psychiatrists to find out which ones are interested and knowledgeable about bipolar disorder. If none is available, you may have to go outside your community to a university hospital or a bigger city to find the doctor who can give your child the best evaluation.

Which doctors receive the most training in bipolar medications?

Psychiatrists receive the best training in bipolar medications. Younger psychiatrists often know more about the biochemistry of the condition, whereas older doctors have more of the experience needed to treat bipolar disorder. Make sure the psychiatrist you choose has some of both.

Should my daughter see a child psychiatrist or a general psychiatrist?

I have heard it argued both ways. Child and adolescent psychiatrists are the doctors who have the most training in treating children, particularly young children. Unfortunately, child and adolescent psychiatrists are in short supply in some areas.

General psychiatrists specializing in bipolar disorder may have seen more cases of bipolar disorder overall, and may be more familiar with its lifetime course. Many psychiatrists have a special interest in psychopharmacology and have sought greater education about medications. Ultimately, it comes down to who is the most qualified doctor in your area and how interested he or she is in educating you and treating your child's bipolar disorder.

How much is enough time for my son and me to spend with the doctor?

I see parents and children for fifty minutes every appointment. This provides enough time to evaluate your child, share important information, teach you about bipolar disorder, and discuss the decisions we must make together. Ultimately, you and your son must become the ones who make the decisions about bipolar treatment. You are in this for the long haul, and you will have to deal with many doctors in a lifetime. You must educate yourselves well enough now so you and your child can eventually steer the ship.

SEVERAL TYPES OF MEDICAL DOCTORS TREAT BIPOLAR DISORDER

In order to pick the right doctor for your child, you need to know the differences among the types of medical doctors who offer bipolar treatment.

What exactly is a psychiatrist? Is he or she a medical doctor or a psychotherapist?

A general psychiatrist is a licensed medical doctor who has specialized training in medications and psychotherapy. A psychiatrist has completed four years of premedical training in college and four years of medical training at a medical university, earning an M.D. (medical doctor) degree and a license to practice all types of medicine. Psychiatrists next complete one year of hands-on training in general medical treatment in an accredited hospital internship. Then they complete three more years of training in a hospital psychiatry residency program, where they learn to prescribe medications and do psychotherapy. Psychiatrists may also choose additional specialized psychiatric training as a chief resident and/or a fellow in a university hospital psychiatric training program or in a subspecialty program like adolescent psychiatry or psychopharmacology. General psychiatrists have received extensive training in the causes, biology, psychology, physiology, and medications for bipolar disorder. They can provide either medications, psychotherapy, or both together. Psychiatrists are often more expensive than other mental health professionals.

How much do general psychiatrists know about bipolar disorder?

General psychiatrists usually have lots of training in bipolar disorder. They may have seen many cases of bipolar disorder and may be especially familiar with the special medications and psychotherapies that are useful for treating bipolar disorder. Some general psychiatrists specialize in treating bipolar disorder.

Aren't there child psychiatrists? What do they do?

Child and adolescent psychiatrists have received training in general psychiatry and then completed an additional two-year program in the care of children with mental and emotional problems. They are the experts in child-hood mental illness. The principles and practices of the American Academy of Child and Adolescent Psychiatry can be found on their organization's Web site, listed on page 252. Child and adolescent psychiatrists have specif-ically devoted their careers to treating children, especially young children, and are familiar with the special mental disorders of childhood, including pervasive developmental disorder, autism, and overanxious disorder of child-hood. There are relatively few child and adolescent psychiatrists compared with a large demand. Child and adolescent psychiatrists often charge more than other psychiatrists.

In this book, when I say "psychiatrist," I will assume that you know that this could be a general psychiatrist or a child and adolescent psychiatrist.

I heard of a psychiatric psychopharmacologist who has short appointments. What's that?

A psychiatric psychopharmacologist is a psychiatrist specializing in prescrib-ing medicine for psychiatric disorders. They may have graduated from a psychiatric training program that stresses medication education, and they may have acquired extra education and training in the use of psychiatric med-ications. Many do not offer psychotherapy.

Are psychiatrists the only medical doctors who treat bipolar disorder?

Both pediatricians and family practice doctors receive training in the treat-ment of psychiatric disorders, including bipolar disorder. These doctors may be quite practiced at treating unipolar major depression, but most of those that I know prefer to turn bipolar disorder over to psychiatrists.

HOW TO FIND A GOOD DOCTOR IN YOUR AREA

Fortunately, there are many good doctors with education and experi-ence in treating bipolar disorder who can help your child. Unfortunately,

SKILLS TO LOOK FOR IN CHOOSING A DOCTOR FOR YOUR BIPOLAR CHILD

• • • • • •

- Your doctor must be a good *diagnostician*. The doctor must be aware of the diagnostic criteria for bipolar and other disorders and be able to apply them objectively. Diagnoses made by first impressions or gut feelings are not helpful for your bipolar child.
- Your doctor should have good *clinical experience* that can only be obtained by diagnosing and successfully treating hundreds or more children suffering from bipolar disorder.
- Your doctor should be a good *physician and healer* in the broadest sense of the word. He or she should be able to supply you and your child with reassurance, inspiration, and a desire to do what is necessary to be healthy.
- Your doctor should be a good *pharmacologist* who reads the medical literature and has plenty of experience treating bipolar children with medicine. Your doctor needs to know more than what is in the textbooks.
- Whether you ask your psychiatrist to provide your child's psychotherapy or not, your doctor must be an accomplished *psychotherapist* with a knowledge of and training in proven therapies (see Chapter 6) in order to understand your child's psychological makeup, to develop good communication, to help allay your child's fears, and to help both of you maintain the best attitude for your child's health and happiness.
- Your doctor should be a good enough *internist* to be aware of your child's internal physical health and to know when to refer problems to your pediatrician, family doctor, or specialist.
- Your doctor must be a good person and a good *role model,* in order to help with your child's physical, mental, and emotional growth. Sometimes the strength of his or her personality may be the most important thing helping your child make it through tough, stressful periods before the medications start working.

psychiatrists are not distributed evenly across the country, with the greatest concentration found in New York City and the larger cities in southern California. Nevertheless, wherever you live, I believe that you *can* find a doctor who can help your child. To locate a good psychiatrist, ask your current primary care physician, pediatrician, and any other doctors you trust to recommend a psychiatrist with whom they have worked. Ask friends and relatives with children in treatment how much they like their child's psychiatrist. Go to local and Internet bipolar support groups, where you will have an opportunity to interact with psychiatrists and hear other parents discuss what they like and dislike about their doctors. You can find out more on this in Chapter 12.

What if the psychiatrist I want to see has a long waiting list or I can't get an appointment?

In this situation, you need a referral from a local colleague who can convince the prospective psychiatrist to see your child. Ask any of your current doctors if they will call the psychiatrist or ask any other medical professionals you know if they will call and recommend your child for treatment. If you cannot find a referring doctor, see if you know one of the doctor's current patients who will ask the doctor to see you. Be patient and be prepared to make yourself available if there are cancellations at the last minute.

Can I ask a specialist to meet with me and my son once or twice and give me his or her opinion?

Absolutely. Most psychiatrists will agree to provide a consultation or second opinion to evaluate your son and suggest possible treatments without any commitment to take your child as their patient.

What should I ask a psychiatrist in order to decide whether I want him or her to treat my bipolar son?

I recommend asking whether the doctor has an interest in and feels comfortable treating childhood bipolar disorder. You can ask how many bipolar patients the doctor has seen in his or her career and how many the doctor is currently seeing. You should ask the doctor about his or her treatment philosophy for childhood bipolar disorder. If he is a young psychiatrist, you may ask how long he has been practicing psychiatry, and if he is a gray-haired physician, you may ask whether he is up-to-date and comfortable with the new medicines for treating bipolar disorder.

What else can I check?

You can check to make sure the psychiatrist has a current medical license in good standing by looking on the Internet Web page of your state medical licensing board. You may ask where your prospective psychiatrist went to medical school and where he or she completed his or her psychiatric residency. Good education often predicts a good physician.

What can I do to find out if a psychiatrist is the right match for me and my girl?

For this, you will have to see how you and your daughter feel when you are together with the psychiatrist in his or her office. If it seems like good chemistry, this doctor may be right for you and your daughter.

AT THE APPOINTMENT

For the first appointment, it is a good idea to write down any questions you have for the psychiatrist so you will not forget them. If you have time, it would be useful to write down the names of any medications given to your child in the past, when they were given, and how your child responded. If your daughter cycles, the psychiatrist will love it if you bring in a Life Events Table (see Chapter 2). If your child has had other evaluations and testing, bring reports for the psychiatrist to see. However, it is okay to ask the psychiatrist what he or she thinks before showing other people's opinions if you do not want the new doctor to be influenced by previous assessments.

Q **Will I have to pay for my son's evaluation appointment if we don't continue going to see her?**

The psychiatrist will expect you to pay for the time spent on your son's evaluation appointment, even if you do not come back.

Q **What will happen to me and my daughter in our first appointment with a psychiatrist?**

This is quite variable and depends on the individual psychiatrist. I can only give you an example from my own practice. In general, I would ask you and your daughter to come half an hour early to complete paperwork and psychological testing. Then I would meet with you and your daughter, separately or together, depending on your daughter's age. I would try to get an understanding of the history of the condition, and conduct a psychiatric examination of your girl. Usually this will be based on an interview with both of you. I might ask you to have the results of your daughter's last physical examination faxed to me with her latest blood tests or I might ask you to get additional blood tests, to test for physical problems that could affect your child's emotions. I would try to complete this phase of the examination in one fifty-minute appointment, but sometimes I need two or more appointments to gather enough information for my opinion. Then I will discuss with you what I think is going on with your daughter and what treatment options are likely to help her.

Q **Should I come alone to the first appointment or bring my son?**

It depends on you. You might prefer to come alone to your son's first evaluation appointment so you can discuss your son's problems without interruption.

What tests can help me be sure that my son really has bipolar disorder?

Whether your son has bipolar disorder depends on whether he matches the official bipolar diagnostic criteria of the *American Psychiatric Association's Diagnostic and Statistical Manual* (see Chapter 2 and Appendix 1) and what your doctor finds on his or her evaluation. Doctors might give your son psych tests like the Mood Disorders Questionnaire, the Petterson Mania Rating Scale, the Hamilton Scales of Depression and Anxiety, and others to measure your son's symptoms, but tests cannot determine his diagnosis. Although you may hear otherwise, there are no blood tests, EEGs, or brain-imaging tests that can diagnose or rule out bipolar disorder in your son.

What is neuropsych testing? How can it help my child?

Neuropsych testing can evaluate your child's mental abilities in the areas of attention, memory, speech, language, spatial relations, abstract thinking, and sequential, stepwise thinking. The results can help pinpoint what areas of the brain are not functioning correctly and they can suggest helpful medical and psychotherapy treatments to correct the problem. I perform neuropsych testing in my office if it is indicated, but many psychiatrists send children out to be tested by a neuropsychologist.

I took my daughter to the doctor, who made a diagnosis and prescribed some medicine. Now he wants us to come back to his office and pay for another appointment. Why?

To begin treatment, it may take your doctor one to six months before finding the right medication, to increase it slowly to a therapeutic dose, and to

solve any remaining problems that your daughter may have. Your psychiatrist may ask your daughter to return every one or two weeks during the
initial phases of treatment.

After your daughter is stabilized, your psychiatrist will want to follow
her regularly, probably every month, for the first year. Your doctor will not
expect you to handle your daughter's medical treatment on your own.

What is the doctor looking for when we come for our regular appointments?

The doctor may be looking at any or all of these: abstract thinking, activity, agitation, appearance, attention, expression, logic, memory, perception,
posture, sequential thought processing, speech, suicidal thoughts, thought
content, thought patterns, and emotions including anger, anxiety, boredom, calmness, elation, emptiness, fear, hopelessness, irritability, loneliness,
panic, peacefulness, and sadness. These provide clues to your child's inner
well-being and response to treatment. The doctor will also want to know
about changes in your child's activity, behavior, eating habits, homework,
schoolwork, sleep, socializing, and stress levels.

The psychiatrist gave my son a prescription for 200 mg of carbamazepine and he seems to be doing better. Why would she want to increase his dose?

Most psychiatrists will want to start your son out at very low doses to make
sure he has no side effects and to give his body a chance to get used to the
medications. Even if your son looks better to you, he may still be a long
way from his most normal, natural self. Expect most psychiatrists to adjust
the medication dose between two and five times before reaching the level
that is ideal for your child.

Q Why won't my psychiatrist ever give my son more than a month's worth of medicine?

We are taught in medical school not to give more than one month's supply of medicine to depressed children. Suicidal depressed children often choose to kill themselves by overdosing on their prescription medications. Consequently, we try to limit the amount of medication so that there will never be enough to kill your son if he should somehow swallow all the pills in his bottle. Another reason we limit the amount prescribed is to help us keep track of how much medicine you have and how much your son has been taking. Furthermore, there are often legal or medical concerns that determine prescribing policies.

Q Why do I have to drag my girl to see the doctor? Why can't I just talk to him on the telephone?

In my experience, treating children over the telephone just does not work. I usually need to see and interact with the child for twenty minutes or more to get a good idea of his or her current condition and progress. That's why I require children and parents to see me personally for prescriptions and to make any changes in care.

Q How can we reduce the costs of bipolar treatment for our daughter?

The only realistic way to reduce the costs of bipolar treatment is to help stabilize your daughter's bipolar disorder and help her return to her most normal, natural self as soon as possible. The costs of uncontrolled bipolar disorder vastly outweigh the costs of treatment.

Q I have a doctor but I am dissatisfied with my daughter's treatment. What should I do?

This is the time to seek a second opinion. For consultation, you want an experienced psychiatrist who has completed psychiatric residency training at a good university. Don't be afraid to ask your own physician to suggest the best expert in the area. Your current doctor should have no hesitation in helping you find a second opinion. In fact, most doctors will welcome it.

Q How do I know when it is the right time to seek a second opinion?

I always say that the right time to get a second opinion is the moment when you start wondering whether you should get a second opinion.

Q I've taken my son to four doctors and they each say something different. Whom should I believe?

Many psychiatrists find the diagnosis of bipolar disorder challenging, especially if they have not seen many cases, or have trained in a small hospital. A doctor's track record in successfully treating bipolar children like your son is the most important indicator that the doctor knows what he is talking about. If the psychiatrist is a bipolar specialist, so much the better. Otherwise, you have to go with the doctor that you feel you can trust.

Q Are there fraudulent practitioners out there? How can I tell?

Steer clear of practitioners who imply that other professionals are no good and that only *they* can help your child. Avoid practitioners who sell their own medications, who promise results, or who pressure you to sign up and pay in advance for a series of appointments.

I never went to medical school. How can I be sure what is best for my bipolar son?

There is so much ignorance and misinformation floating around that you must become an expert on your son's bipolar disorder. You are already learning by reading this book. In addition, ask your doctor questions, go to support groups, find out what other parents have learned, and attend bipolar organizations' meetings and conferences. Chapter 12 will help you.

4.

A Healthy Lifestyle Can Improve Your Child's Bipolar Disorder

. . . .

Based on my clinical experience, I estimate that, when bipolar medications and therapy are optimal, changing lifestyle and health patterns can reduce residual symptoms by 10 to 30 percent. Best of all, lifestyle changes are easy to make, safe, and completely free. The most important are getting proper sleep, promoting good eating habits, proper exercising, scheduling daily activities, and reducing stress.

THE RIGHT AMOUNT OF SLEEP FOR YOUR BIPOLAR CHILD

Sleep and bipolar disorder are tied closely together in children. Bipolar disorder causes sleep problems, and poor sleep drives bipolar disorder. Helping your bipolar child get proper sleep is a tough challenge. The physiological effects of bipolar disorder interfere with normal sleep and, when sleep is abnormal, your child ends up sleep-deprived and exhausted. When you try to enforce sleeping and waking times, you are inviting big fights at bedtime and in the morning, especially in younger children. However, by setting up and enforcing schedules of sleep, meals, and activity we can get the body back on track—sleeping at night and staying awake during the day.

What is it with sleep? First, my son can't go
to sleep and days later, all he wants to
do is sleep.

Many children with bipolar disorder have reversed sleep and wake cycles
so that their body thinks it is daytime at night and nighttime during the
day. This results in staying up late at night and wanting to sleep all day (in
bipolar depression) or staying up late at night and staying up all day too
(in bipolar mania).

Can my bipolar son go to bed late on
weekends? He sleeps late in the morning.

When a child goes to sleep too late at night, sleeping longer in the morning does not fix the problem. In fact, if your son is sleepy when he finally
wakes up, it may be a sign that the quality of his late morning sleep is poor
and not restful. Restful sleep occurs at night.

Can insomnia trigger a bipolar episode?

I have frequently seen sleep deprivation worsen bipolar depression or even
trigger the onset of mania. Unfortunately, some doctors advise twenty-four-
hour sleep deprivation as a cure for sleep problems *and* depression. These
approaches are not good for your bipolar child.

What time do you recommend that my son
go to sleep at night?

For younger children, bedtimes of 8:00 to 9:00 p.m. are reasonable. I advise
adolescents with bipolar disorder to try going to bed at 10:00 p.m. every
night for a week to see if they feel much better (they usually do). To give

this an honest try, your son must be in bed with the lights out and no media or telephone by 10:00 p.m. on weekdays *and* weekends.

What do you recommend doing to help my child get to sleep at night?

Bipolar children often feel activated at night, rather than during the day, with increased physical energy and active thoughts. This is called a reversed-sleeping cycle, and it usually improves when bipolar medications are optimum. To be able to fall asleep at night, your child should be up early in the morning, not take any daytime naps, and go to bed with the lights out at the same time each night.

Pay attention to what doctors call "sleep hygiene." Make sure that the room is dark and quiet. Some bipolar children cannot sleep in the same room with brothers and sisters, and end up sleeping in another room or on the couch at night. Try to ensure that the room is not too hot at night; if the weather is cold, make sure your child has plenty of covers. Reserve the bed for sleeping only and discourage your child from reading or studying in bed. Do not put a television or computer in the room with the bed because the temptation to stay up will be too great. If your child wakes in the middle of the night, insist that he or she go back to bed and not start any activities. If these tricks do not work, ask your doctor for help.

Is there anything over the counter that I can give my child to help her sleep?

It is never advisable to rely on any medications to get to sleep. However, sometimes it is necessary. If you must give your child an occasional sleep aid, see if your doctor recommends diphenhydramine (Benadryl). It is available in almost every drugstore as an allergy medication, in brand name and generic, and its effect is usually predictable. Try giving your child one tablet of diphenhydramine, following the age recommendations on the label, when she just cannot get to sleep.

Some children cannot tolerate diphenhydramine; they feel sedated the next day. I have very occasionally heard of children who responded to Benadryl with excitement or agitation. In most of these cases, the diphenhydramine dose was paired with a decongestant, which increases adrenaline levels. Make sure that you buy a product that contains diphenhydramine only and, if you have any questions, check with your doctor.

DIET AND NUTRITION

Diet and nutrition are important for children with bipolar disorder. Every bipolar child needs to have vitamins, nutrients, and sufficient protein in their diet, as well as minimum fat for good health. Also, I agree with the mother who first pointed out that her child's tantrums mainly occurred between meals, when her child was hungry.

How can I make sure my daughter gets enough of the basic vitamins she needs?

Most vitamins can be obtained in meals, but because of bipolar disorder, your child may need additional supplementation. If your child is a picky eater and does not consume many green vegetables, she may need extra folate, which is an important vitamin for nervous system function. If your daughter does not eat orange vegetables like carrots, she may need supplementation with vitamin A (beta-carotene). If she does not drink milk or does not go outside in the sunshine enough, she may need supplemental vitamin D. There are two kinds of vitamin D, ergocalciferol (D_2) and cholecalciferol (D_3). Cholecalciferol is more active and has been shown to prevent fractures, so it is the better choice when evaluating supplements. Vitamins B_6 (pyridoxine) and B_{12} (cyanocobalamin) are also particularly important for nervous system function, and deficiencies in these vitamins can sometimes produce symptoms that somewhat resemble bipolar disorder. For more information on vitamin and herb supplements, see Chapter 12.

I heard that bipolar disorder was caused by diet and could be cured by diet.

First let me state conclusively that, despite what you have heard from "experts," there is no acceptable scientific research study that shows the slightest detectable benefit for any therapeutic diet in bipolar disorder. Period.

I read about diets that recommend different amounts of protein, carbohydrates, and fats. How do these affect my daughter's bipolar disorder, anyway?

Here is what I know at this time. Your daughter needs ample protein, raw green and orange vegetables, vitamins, and other nutrients. Unfortunately, it may be difficult for your daughter to get ideal nutrition if she has strong eating preferences or if she is a picky eater. Older children tell me they feel better when they are getting enough protein in their diet (25 to 55 grams daily), whereas they often report feeling manic symptoms after eating chocolate and large, starchy, fatty meals.

How can I make sure my child gets plenty of protein?

This is easy. You can give them steak, chicken, turkey, fish, eggs, nonfat milk, nonfat yogurt, nonfat cottage cheese, nonfat farmer's cheese, and tofu. Salads with raw vegetables and protein are good meals for both lunch and dinner.

Do you think we should limit the amount of carbohydrates our bipolar son eats?

At this moment, I encourage you to feed your child plenty of protein and vegetables and to limit starch. Starches and fats account for most of the foods bipolar individuals associate with hyperactivity. Unfortunately, feeding children starch seems to have become a national pastime, and children are barraged with advertisements for morning fare like breakfast food cereals, bagels, croissants, doughnuts, muffins, and toast. Lunch and dinner meals of pasta, pizza, garlic rolls, cakes, and pies are promoted over the radio and television. Fast food is inextricably associated with bread, breading, buns, corn chips, pancakes, potatoes, tortillas, and waffles. Even health food store supplements and "health power bars" are loaded with starch. Limiting your child's intake may not be easy, but the rewards should be worth the struggle.

In addition, excess weight gain is a common problem for many children today and, unfortunately, it is especially common for bipolar sufferers. By bringing starch intake under control, you will help your bipolar child reduce risk for obesity and its consequences: diabetes, heart disease, and stroke.

Does sugar cause mania?

There is a general belief that sugar amps up bipolar children and that older children crave it for that reason. This is actually easy to disprove in your home. Offer your bipolar daughter a spoonful of white table sugar (supposedly the worst kind of sugar), and see what happens. I have never found a bipolar child who was interested. Then, see what happens if you can get your children to eat the table sugar. If your experience is like mine, you will see no effect of any kind. It is too bad, because it would make life easier if something simple like sugar was actually the cause of our children's problems.

Is there any specific food that people with bipolar disorder link to hyperactivity?

Chocolate is the food most bipolar children and adults believe causes a hyperactive reaction. In the early days of psychiatry, chocolate cravings were part of a condition called hysteroid dysphoria that was also characterized by fatigue, sadness, sleepiness, and weight gain. Today, we would call it bipolar depression. Chocolate contains stimulants in the form of caffeine, phenylethylamine, theobromine, and theophylline, which have been known to trigger manic episodes by increasing brain adrenaline.

What should my bipolar daughter have for breakfast?

I encourage everyone to get at least half of their 25-to-55-gram total daily protein requirement at breakfast, so that they can use it for the rest of the day. For breakfast, your child can eat eggs, nonfat yogurt, nonfat cottage cheese, leftover chicken, and pressed low-fat turkey. If you are buying dairy or other packaged food, it is easy to gauge the amount of protein: just look on the side of the package where the percentage of daily protein requirements is listed.

What's the best schedule for my bipolar daughter's meals?

I encourage your daughter to have three usual meals, breakfast, lunch, and dinner. These should be eaten at about the same time every day and the amount of food consumed should be about the same every day. Bipolar children who need to eat more frequently can have vegetables and fruit at regular intervals.

Is reading health magazines enough for me to know what foods are healthy?

Actually, much of the information available in magazines, Internet sites, television commercials, and nutrition stores is inadequate or even misleading. The reason is simple. Whenever there is money to be made, you cannot trust health information. When magazines, Internet sites, commercials, and health food stores are promoting products that they help sell, then you cannot rely on their information. For example, commercials and salesclerks will tell you that health and power bars are good to eat but most are no different than candy bars with a different wrapper and a higher price. Food faddism goes in both directions. For example, fast-food restaurants are vilified even though they may be a source of salad or fruit that your child will eat. If you are unsure, consult a professional nutritionist and/or buy a college nutrition textbook.

Q Everybody knows you should drink water daily for health. Does my bipolar child need more than the average recommended intake?

Plants and bipolar children should not be overwatered. Unless it is hot outside or your child has a fever, drinking reasonable amounts of fluids during the day is usually sufficient. However, drinking too *much* water can wash away the water-soluble vitamins and electrolytes your child needs and can also dilute the levels of bipolar medications, lowering doses to the point that they are no longer therapeutic. It is better to follow the edict "Everything in moderation."

Q What should I do about my bipolar son's nutrition? His eating habits are terrible.

The strongest weapon in the war for your son's good nutrition is the behavior of the other members of your family. When parents and siblings eat healthy meals and snacks, your son is more likely to join in. Protein, fruit, and raw vegetables at regularly scheduled meals and low-calorie fruits and vegetables available in the house will help set your son's eating habits inside and outside your home. However, if you have chocolate, ice cream, and candy bars at home, you are just asking for trouble. You cannot expect your bipolar son to eat healthily if his family members are wolfing down junk food.

Weight and Weight Loss

Weight problems are an ongoing challenge for bipolar children and their parents. Both severe overweight, with its attendant problems of diabetes and heart disease, and extreme underweight, accompanied by failure to develop normally, pose potential problems. Bipolar disorder can interfere with children's weight by driving their metabolism up or down, altering their appetite, and producing rigid, resistant eating behaviors. Usually children eat more when depressed and less when activated, although either is possible when symptoms are mixed.

How can I tell if my son is at the right weight?

In our weight-conscious culture, everyone has a different view about what is right. If your son looks like his parents or grandparents did at that age, his weight may be normal for his inherited body type. At your next appointment with your son's pediatrician or family doctor, ask him or her to weigh your son and compare that weight with charts of average weight and height to see if he is within the healthy range. You might want to ask for a copy of the chart for your own use, if your doctor has extras.

Tommy is a very picky eater and he is losing weight. What can I do?

Many young bipolar children have picky, inflexible eating habits that contribute to being underweight. Start with trying to find food that your son will eat. Until he reaches a normal weight, feel free to feed him high-calorie foods containing a lot of protein like ice cream, milk shakes, and cheese (avoiding starches, if possible). As long as you and the rest of your family are healthy eaters, you can transition your son to more nutritious fare when he returns to a normal weight.

My daughter started losing weight and now she is so skinny she looks like a boy. Help!

Extreme thinness is more common in bipolar children than in the rest of the population and, in addition to picky eating, it can be caused by starving oneself to lose weight, vomiting to lose weight, or overexercising. In girls who have started having their periods, missing menstrual cycles or cessation of menstruation are often signs of malnutrition. If your daughter's weight has dropped 15 percent or more from her ideal weight, then her condition is severe. Discuss this problem with her therapist and psychiatrist, and look on the Internet for more information on eating disorders. Look into nutritional counseling, a therapist specializing in eating disorders, and eating-disorder programs.

My bipolar son is overweight. Should I be concerned?

Your bipolar son is more likely to be overweight than other children, especially if he is depressed. By the time they reach adulthood, 35 percent of bipolar children will be overweight and 25 percent will be obese. Because of this obesity, they will be at greater risk of heart problems and twice as likely to have diabetes. Ten percent of them will grow up to have adult-onset (type 2) diabetes.

What types of meals are best for my overweight bipolar daughter?

If you schedule the heaviest meals early in the day, your child will have an opportunity to burn off the calories before bedtime. Try to schedule light dinners early in the evening so your child will not go to bed with a full stomach, which promotes weight gain and may worsen bipolar symptoms. Snacks of raw fruit or vegetables may be eaten any time of day.

My doctor said my son's weight is endangering his health. Is there a safe medication for him?

It would be healthy for your son to lower his fat intake. There is a weight-loss medication called orlistat (Xenical and Alli) that works by reducing the absorption of fat from the food your son eats. Orlistat does not interfere with the activity of your son's bipolar medications. Xenical works gradually, but it is more likely than other weight-loss medications to take your son's weight off and keep it off, so be patient. Some individuals experience cramping and loose stools, while others do not. Limiting fat intake will lessen the chance of these side effects. Orlistat can decrease absorption of vitamins A, D, E, and K, so the addition of a multivitamin is a must. Xenical is a prescription drug, while Alli is nonprescription; please ask your doctor before using either one for your bipolar child.

Herbs and Supplements

The health supplements that are promoted so heavily on television and in magazines may not be helpful for your bipolar child and may even make things worse. Also, remember that the FDA does not test or license supplements, so we have no reliable research on their safety. Consult with your physician before trying any new supplement, so you can work together on your child's nutrition.

Can supplements treat my daughter's bipolar disorder?

At this time, there are no treatments except prescription mood stabilizer medications that can make your daughter's dysfunctional bipolar brain cells function normally. Mood stabilizers are the cornerstone of treatment for childhood bipolar disorder and you cannot hope to replace them with other products.

Are there supplements that help bipolar disorder? I heard that something called inositol helps.

Inositol (also called cyclohexanehexol) is an important component of the cell wall membranes in brain cells. Our bodies manufacture inositol, and additional supplies can be obtained from melons, oranges, bran, and supplements. Several studies have found abnormalities of inositol in bipolar patients, and there is even a theory of bipolar disorder called the "inositol hypothesis." Inositol has been tried in bipolar disorder treatment alone and in combination with mood stabilizers, sometimes with helpful results. I cannot say for sure whether inositol will be safe and effective for your child because insufficient studies have been performed, but there is some good research showing that it may be helpful.

What about omega-3 oils?

There have been many claims and some research suggesting that consumption of certain oils might help depression. These include omega-3 fatty acids called EPA (eicosapentaenoic acid) and DHA (docosahexaenoic acid), which are found in fish. Fish oils are recommended by the American Heart Association to prevent heart attacks and lower effects of cholesterol, and they might decrease bipolar symptoms. The best way for your child to get these oils is to eat fish. If that is not possible, your child can try fish oil supplements to see if there is any clear improvement in the way he or she feels. Evening primrose oil has an abundance of linoleic and linolenic acids, which may turn into omega-3 or have additional benefits. Flaxseed, grape seed, and rapeseed oils might have similar properties, but I do not recommend them at this time.

How do I know what doses of vitamins my bipolar child needs?

Children of different ages need different doses of vitamins. You can find good general information on different-aged children's vitamin requirements in Chapter 12. Younger children should take pediatric vitamins, and your doctor can recommend a brand. As children grow into their late teens, they can begin to take adult vitamins. In order to make sure your child receives plenty of vitamins without going overboard, I recommend "once-a-day" vitamins. These small, easy-to-take pills are available inexpensively on sale or as drugstore brands. If you are worried about your teen getting enough vitamins, you can have your child take two "once-a-day" vitamins daily.

The extreme media claims like "depression cured in three minutes" by vitamins are just lies. Furthermore, the large doses of vitamins recommended by some magazines and popular books are usually not helpful and can be harmful. For example, more than 100 mg of B_6 can cause tingling or sensory changes in many children, and high doses of vitamin A (beta-carotene) can be toxic. Always discuss vitamin supplementation with your child's doctor and be wary of "miracle" claims for high-dosage supplements.

What about Saint-John's-wort? Would it help my daughter with her bipolar depression?

I have seen Saint-John's-wort worsen bipolar depression and trigger mania and have read reports of it doing so. I would never recommend giving it to your daughter.

I read that something called 5-HT can prevent depression. Should we include it in our bipolar child's vitamin regimen?

"5-HT" is the scientific abbreviation for serotonin (also called 5-hydroxy-tryptamine), which you might have heard of in conjunction with the dangers of antidepressants in bipolar disorder (see chapters 1 and 5). Theoretically, oral serotonin could worsen bipolar depression, trigger mania and psychosis, and worsen the life course of the disorder. However, I suspect that most oral serotonin is broken down in the stomach and does nothing but deplete your pocketbook.

I read that chromium helps with depression. Should I give it to my son?

Chromium picolinate can produce changes in neurochemicals important to bipolar disorder such as adrenaline, and dopamine (see Chapter 1), as well as serotonin, and it can act somewhat like insulin. However, these changes are neither predictable nor controlled because the potency and strength of chromium supplements varies so much. Some forms of oral chromium (other than chromium picolinate) have been associated with liver failure and lung cancer. I recommend keeping chromium away from your son until we know more about its safety and effectiveness.

Are there any natural supplements that will
help my son sleep?

Valerian is a plant extract that has been used for hundreds of years to make
people sleepy at bedtime. It may work by blocking the effects of an important major nervous system neurochemical involved in alertness (called
acetylcholine, or ACh). So far, I have not seen this herb cause problems in
bipolar disorder. Try giving your son valerian one or two hours before bedtime under your doctor's supervision. Lemon balm (*Melissa officinalis*) and
passionflower (*Passiflora incarnata*) are herbs that also cause sleepiness, but
their effect on bipolar disorder has not been studied.

What about DMAE? Does it do anything to
help bipolar disorder?

DMAE (also called deanol or dimethylaminoethanol) helps increase the alertness neurochemical acetylcholine (ACh). DMAE promotes alertness and
mental energy, and it was once licensed as a treatment for hyperactivity in children (although it was later withdrawn for lack of efficacy data). DMAE may
be helpful for bipolar disorder; however, a few cases have appeared in the medical literature claiming that DMAE triggered mania and depression, so I do not
recommend DMAE for bipolar children until this issue has been clarified.

My bipolar depressed daughter is always tired.
I read great things about ginseng. Is it
safe? The clerk at the vitamin store
recommended it highly.

Panax ginseng (Korean ginseng or red ginseng) is a stimulant that can increase the blood levels of medications such as olanzapine (Zyprexa), clozapine (Clozaril), trazodone (Desyrel), and others. In large doses, I have seen
Panax ginseng trigger bipolar episodes so severe that they require hospitalization. I do not consider it safe for bipolar children.

Q Kava is an age-old natural herb used for relaxation. Would it help my child feel less anxious and wound up?

Kava has been associated with liver toxicity, and I suspect that it will soon be off the market. I do not recommend that anyone—bipolar or not—take this herb.

Q Several health professionals have offered to sell me glandular extracts to improve my young girl's mood and energy. Do they work?

Dried and pulverized animal glands have been used for centuries. However, these products typically have little if any potency by the time they reach your child. In fact, I find the whole idea rather revolting. Avoid them.

Q Are the herbs and supplements sold on the Internet safe?

Right now, the Internet is unpoliced, and there is no way of predicting what you will be sent in the mail. Supplements sold on the Internet have been found to have no active ingredients, impotent ingredients, unwanted prescription medications, and dirt. I recommend that you find a legitimate pharmacy or health food store you can trust and buy your supplements in person.

EXERCISE

I believe that exercise is an important part of bipolar treatment both to help keep your child physically healthy and to help keep bipolar disorder under control. Unfortunately, bipolar children often become obsessive about exercising or are encouraged to exercise too much. In addition, some bipolar children use exercise to destabilize their bipolar disorder in hopes of getting a manic energy boost. Help your child develop a scheduled exercise program that is not too extreme in either direction.

How much exercise do you recommend?

For children who do not already participate in athletic activity, I recommend twenty minutes of hard exercise every day of the week. It may not be easy to persuade your child to exercise, especially if he or she is depressed; however, the long-term benefits are well worth the struggle. Get creative and enlist his or her help doing chores around the house or yard, helping a neighbor, walking the dog, or just playing a game one-on-one. With a reluctant child, it's best to work up to the targeted exercise goal.

I'm a busy bipolar teen. How can I possibly fit one more thing into my day?

Scheduled exercise is one of the important tools you can use to help stabilize your own bipolar disorder. Regular exercise provides a strong cue for setting internal biological clocks. When you have decided on your exercise program, try to schedule your activities at about the same time every day. It is a lot of extra trouble, but I think that if you try for one month to schedule your exercise and other key parts of your life, you will notice that you feel better and that your life is going more smoothly.

Doesn't exercise cure depression? I read it in a magazine.

I wish life were that simple. Exercise stimulates the release of narcotic-like molecules (endorphins) and steroid stress hormones. For many people without bipolar disorder, the release of these molecules and hormones may temporarily lift their mood. Unfortunately, too many endorphins and steroids stress hormones can worsen bipolar disorder. This is why it's important to exercise in moderation.

My daughter is exercising for hours every day
and she says she's feeling super. Can too
much exercise make her manic?

Yes, overexercise can trigger mania in your daughter, by increasing the release of endorphins and cortisol. If your daughter is manic, she may begin
to exercise even more to relieve the agitation that accompanies her high-
energy state.

I want my bipolar son to be a star athlete.
Will bipolar disorder get in the way?

The stress from the pressure to win may worsen your son's bipolar disorder,
especially at critical times of the year. Moreover, being a star athlete takes
time away from school, studying, and a normal social life. For kids with bipolar disorder it may be better to stick with moderate exercise and minimal
pressure, while emphasizing good grades, so your child has a great future.

My daughter's ballet teacher is working her to
death. He says she can be a professional.

You cannot trust dance teachers or coaches to know what is good for your
daughter's bipolar disorder. I prefer that your daughter stay healthy, have a
fun childhood, and develop a firm foundation for her future in school instead
of being pushed to her limit.

What do you think about sports drinks or
power drinks and my bipolar disorder?

Sports and power drinks usually contain stimulants such as caffeine or stimulating herbs that can destabilize your bipolar disorder. Also, these drinks have
little or no nutritional value. If you check the labels, you will find that most

of these drinks are just water with sugars like sucrose, fructose, and corn syrup.

THE DAILY SCHEDULE PROGRAM FOR YOUR CHILD'S BIPOLAR DISORDER

We may not give much thought to our daily schedules; however, they dramatically affect how we feel and function. In medical school, we learned that missing sleep and missing meals could trigger seizures in epileptics. A few years later, I noticed that the same things could trigger manic episodes in bipolar patients. I also realized that my bipolar depressed patients were describing symptoms similar to jet lag, which occurs when the body's internal clock becomes out of sync when crossing time zones. It was a "Eureka!" moment. I realized that, by synchronizing the body's internal biological rhythms through strict scheduling of sleep, meals, and exercise, we could decrease bipolar symptoms of both mania and depression.

What is the point of all this scheduling? How does it help my son?

Bipolar disorder has a lot to do with biological cycles. The body's central biological clock is located in the brain (at the so-called suprachiasmatic nucleus). It sets all the body's clocks and biorhythms according to the length of the day. When day length changes with the seasons (or due to daylight saving time), or when there are many cloudy or rainy days without sunlight, your son's internal clocks may get out of synchronization, and body processes like sleep and those involving blood sugar may not run at the right time. You may have experienced this condition of desynchronized internal clocks if you have ever suffered from jet lag, which occurs when your internal biological clocks do not match the outside time because you have traveled into a different time zone. If you have ever had bad jet lag, you know it is a heavy, hungover feeling where you just cannot be your best. This is often what bipolar children describe when the day length changes or the sun is not around to set their body's biological clocks. Scheduling daily events helps your son's body know what time it is and helps keep your son's biological clocks and body rhythms together and running on time.

Why should I put my child on a schedule?

Putting your child on a schedule of sleep, meals, and exercise is a great way to help stabilize bipolar disorder. It may be the best thing you as a parent can do to help keep your child's bipolar disorder under control. Furthermore, teaching your child to operate under a daily activities schedule will help him or her maintain healthy lifestyle habits as an adult. Best of all, it is safe and free. To make scheduling easier, I've written a Daily Schedule Program work sheet for you to use (see page 79).

How can I use the Daily Schedule Program to help my bipolar daughter?

As long as your daughter can read and tell time, the Daily Schedule Program (DSP) can help her. First, carefully remove the Daily Schedule Program work sheet from the book and make several copies. Then sit down with your child and write down the times you want her to wake up, eat breakfast, lunch, and dinner, exercise, and go to bed. Think about these times as you plan them, because you may have to adapt parts of *your* schedule to fit in with your daughter's new schedule. Post the DSP work sheet in a prominent place (such as the kitchen) where everyone can see it. Each day your daughter has to write down the actual times she woke up, ate meals, exercised, and went to bed. Initially, you may have to help her fill out the schedule or have her bring you the schedule to check. When she becomes reliable at following the schedule, you may let her just check the box when the scheduled activity is completed on time.

In order to keep scheduling from becoming a chore, do not take on this job by yourself. Enlist your child's help in preparing his or her own schedule. Get your spouse, other children, grandparents, babysitters, and everyone else to help maintain the schedule. Embrace the schedule yourself and your child may follow your lead.

How do I get my daughter to keep to the Daily Schedule Program?

You may have to help your daughter keep to the schedule at first. If necessary, lead her to bed at night and pull her out of bed in the morning. While your daughter is at home, you can make sure that she has her breakfast, lunch, and dinner at the agreed-on times. Scheduling her exercise may be easy to do if she has sports practices that start and end on time. If not, try to get her to exercise for twenty minutes close to the scheduled time every day. How close is close? I suggest that each scheduled activity not differ more than ten minutes from day to day.

What if my son and I want to change the schedule?

You can make a new DSP work sheet each week until you and your son are satisfied with the schedule. Then copy this Daily Schedule Program work sheet to use every week. When the schedule changes because of summer, vacation, holidays, and so forth, simply fill out a new DSP work sheet and use it.

Should we keep old copies of the Daily Schedule Program?

It is a good idea to keep old copies of the DSP work sheets. These work sheets serve as a record (especially when used in conjunction with the Life Events Table, page 34) of your child's ups and downs. Perhaps your child felt better on a schedule you used several months ago, or perhaps he or she felt worse. Your schedule record can help you and your child find the best fit for feeling great.

What do I talk about with my son when we look at the work sheets together?

When you look at the work sheets with your son, ask him how he has been feeling and see what, if any, improvements resulted from the schedule. These improvements could include being able to get up in the morning, feeling refreshed from a good night's sleep, feeling stronger and more alert from regular exercise, being hungry at mealtime instead of between meals, and so forth.

Do you really think this whole schedule project is worth it? I know I'll get flak from my son.

Try it and see. If you can get your son to buy into the schedule, you will be rewarded by seeing his health improve as he begins to organize his life. When your son grows up, you will get to see him organizing his adult life by using the techniques you taught him when he was a child. This is one of the high points of parenting, when you know that you have helped your son be happier and healthier, and get more out of his life because of your parenting contributions.

THE STRESS CONNECTION

The stress your child experiences at school, at home, and from life in general can worsen his or her bipolar disorder. You can help your child reduce stress by teaching and encouraging the use of relaxation techniques and meditative exercises.

What is stress?

You have heard of the "fight-or-flight reaction." When your child is threatened, angry, or afraid, the body produces an outpouring of potent stimulants

The Daily Schedule Program

You'll Feel Better When Your Life Is Consistent

Write down the scheduled times to wake up, eat meals, exercise, and go to bed. Then each day, write down the actual times you woke up, ate meals, exercised, and went to bed. Later on, you can just check the box if you did your scheduled activity on time.

DATE	DAY	WAKING	BREAKFAST	LUNCH	EXERCISE	DINNER	BED
_____	Monday	planned:	planned:	planned:	planned:	planned:	planned:
		__:__	__:__	__:__	__:__	__:__	__:__
		actual:	actual:	actual:	actual:	actual:	actual:
		☐ __:__	☐ __:__	☐ __:__	☐ __:__	☐ __:__	☐ __:__
_____	Tuesday	planned:	planned:	planned:	planned:	planned:	planned:
		__:__	__:__	__:__	__:__	__:__	__:__
		actual:	actual:	actual:	actual:	actual:	actual:
		☐ __:__	☐ __:__	☐ __:__	☐ __:__	☐ __:__	☐ __:__
_____	Wednesday	planned:	planned:	planned:	planned:	planned:	planned:
		__:__	__:__	__:__	__:__	__:__	__:__
		actual:	actual:	actual:	actual:	actual:	actual:
		☐ __:__	☐ __:__	☐ __:__	☐ __:__	☐ __:__	☐ __:__
_____	Thursday	planned:	planned:	planned:	planned:	planned:	planned:
		__:__	__:__	__:__	__:__	__:__	__:__
		actual:	actual:	actual:	actual:	actual:	actual:
		☐ __:__	☐ __:__	☐ __:__	☐ __:__	☐ __:__	☐ __:__
_____	Friday	planned:	planned:	planned:	planned:	planned:	planned:
		__:__	__:__	__:__	__:__	__:__	__:__
		actual:	actual:	actual:	actual:	actual:	actual:
		☐ __:__	☐ __:__	☐ __:__	☐ __:__	☐ __:__	☐ __:__
_____	Saturday	planned:	planned:	planned:	planned:	planned:	planned:
		__:__	__:__	__:__	__:__	__:__	__:__
		actual:	actual:	actual:	actual:	actual:	actual:
		☐ __:__	☐ __:__	☐ __:__	☐ __:__	☐ __:__	☐ __:__
_____	Sunday	planned:	planned:	planned:	planned:	planned:	planned:
		__:__	__:__	__:__	__:__	__:__	__:__
		actual:	actual:	actual:	actual:	actual:	actual:
		☐ __:__	☐ __:__	☐ __:__	☐ __:__	☐ __:__	☐ __:__
DATE	DAY	WAKING	BREAKFAST	LUNCH	EXERCISE	DINNER	BED

like adrenaline and steroid stress hormones to power the vigorous fighting or running away from danger. In nature, the aggressive physical activity of fight or flight uses up these stimulating neurochemicals. However, in our modern society, which does not allow for vigorous physical fight-or-flight reactions, these potent stimulants build up in the body with no release, causing what doctors and scientists call stress.

For example, if your daughter needs to play harder in a sports game, her body triggers the release of lots of adrenaline and steroid stress hormones into her bloodstream. This allows her to be extra strong and play extra hard. Then, while she is playing hard, her body burns up the high levels of adrenaline and hormones and when the game is over, she feels like herself again. This is what is supposed to happen.

However, if your daughter is waiting in a classroom for a test and her body triggers the release of adrenaline and hormones, there is no activity to burn them up. Instead, she is expected to sit quietly and take the test while her body and mind want to explode. This is biological stress.

Bipolar disorder makes your daughter's body secrete too much adrenaline and steroid stress hormones every day. Then, when a stressful life event triggers the release of even *more* adrenaline and hormones, it is enough to push her bipolar disorder over the edge. These high levels of adrenaline and steroid stress hormones can change her attention, behavior, eating habits, emotions, memory, sleeping, and thinking. This is how stress drives bipolar disorder.

THE STRESS CONNECTION IN BIPOLAR DISORDER

- Stress causes the body to produce extra adrenaline and steroid stress hormones. These stress compounds are carried to the brain and other parts of the body.
- If these stress compounds are not burned up by activity, they overstimulate brain cells that control emotions (amygdala), memory (hippocampus), and activity (brain stem).
- The change in brain cells triggers bipolar episodes, which cause more stress and the release of more adrenaline and steroid stress hormones.

Breaking this cycle is an important step in getting childhood bipolar disorder under control.

What areas of the brain are involved in the stress response?

The brain cells at the top of the head in the HP (hypothalamus-pituitary) area are among the ones that control the production of adrenaline. If the HP area is imbalanced, then adrenaline production can be too high (manic) or too low (depressed). Some doctors think that bipolar disorder results from an imbalance in the HP area of the brain.

Does my son's stress always come from bad things?

No, the stress reaction can be provoked by anything associated with high emotion and anticipation. Stress may be provoked by both weddings and funerals, honors and punishment, good news and bad news.

What's the most likely overlooked source of stress?

Studies show that viral infections cause enough physical stress to destabilize bipolar disorder.

What are some ways I can reduce the effects of stress on my son (and myself)?

If you and your son could completely relax your bodies and quiet your thoughts, the stress cycle would be broken and the effects of stress would melt away. Some of the ways to do this involve relaxation techniques, meditation, and thought stopping.

What is the simplest relaxation technique that you know, and how can I use it?

The simplest technique is simply to breathe slowly in and out while you concentrate on your breath. Try to focus all your attention on your breath as it goes into your body and then keep your focus on it as your breath goes out into the atmosphere. Start doing this for thirty seconds at a time and then increase to one or two minutes. Use this relaxation technique anytime during the day when you have a spare minute and wish to relax. It also makes a wonderful exercise to do at bedtime to help you relax and go to sleep. When you have become familiar with how it works, teach it to your family and anyone else you want to help lighten up and relax.

My daughter is too young to do any techniques. Is there any other way I can quiet and relax her?

Some doctors believe that increasing body temperature has an effect on the central nervous system, and bipolar children often benefit from hot baths. Soaking in hot water may quiet your daughter enough for her to go to sleep at night. Relaxing and soaking in a hot tub may also be a good solution when she is too angry or too sad.

What is the muscle-relaxation method? Is my grade-school daughter too young to do it?

Your daughter can learn and use the muscle-relaxation technique to get to sleep at night, to calm down before homework or sports practice, and to alleviate her tension before a test. You can use it yourself to deal with the stresses of parenting a bipolar child.

The muscle-relaxation technique that I employ has its own script (page 83). Lead your daughter in this exercise a few times until she can do it by

A MUSCLE-RELAXATION TECHNIQUE
FOR YOUR CHILD

Just sit back and close your eyes. I want you to breathe deeply in and out, and every time you breathe in, I want you to imagine that you are gathering up all the stress in your body. When you breathe out you are letting all that stress go out into the atmosphere.

Let's start with your feet and ankles. Tighten the muscles there as hard as you can while you breathe in slowly. Hold your breath. Now relax your muscles as you breathe out all the stress that was in your feet and ankles. Now tighten all the muscles in your thighs, hips, and stomach as hard as you can while you breathe in slowly. Hold your breath. Now relax and breathe all that stress out into the atmosphere. Next, breathe in and tighten all the muscles in your arms and shoulders as hard as you can. Hold your breath. Now, breathe out slowly and release all that tension. Finally, tighten all the muscles in your neck and head and breathe in hard. Hold your breath for a moment and then relax as you release all that stress. Relax and enjoy that feeling for a while.

herself. Rather than try to explain the role of stress, just emphasize the good feeling she will have at the end of the exercise.

What is meditation and what does it do?

Meditation refers to exercises that change the way you think and experience and process information, allowing your body and conscious mind to relax into a more peaceful, calm, and relaxed state. Concentration meditation involves directing the flow of thoughts onto a target in a way that quiets mental activity and relaxes the body.

Are there simple meditations you recommend that can help my bipolar child?

I have reproduced a Meditation Page on page 84 that you can use to teach your child to relax. Carefully remove the Meditation Page from this book. Put the page on a flat surface and read it to your child.

THE MEDITATION PAGE

Remove this page and place it where you can easily use it to reduce stress.

Look at the two lines and notice that there is a place where they cross. Pretend that this place is a black hole. Focus every bit of your attention on this black hole. Whenever you become distracted by a thought, just put it into the black hole and it will be sucked away. Then go back to focusing all your attention on the place where the lines cross.

Start your child doing the exercise for thirty seconds at a time. With more practice, your child will be able to spend more time focusing on the cross and less time being distracted by unwanted thoughts. This increased ability to control thoughts will help your child stay focused in his daily life.

Make copies of the Meditation Page. Put one on your child's desk to help her relax and regain focus while working on homework. Put one by the bed to help her calm down and fall asleep. When your child is upset or having a tantrum, consider asking her to go to her room and use the Meditation Page until she is calm again. Older children and teens may use the page on their own to calm down in emotional situations. It works equally well for anger, anxiety, depression, jealousy, and resentment. As long as your child can focus, the page can be used as a tool.

My daughter and I think the Meditation Page is fun. How does it help her bipolar disorder?

Using the Meditation Page allows your daughter's mind and body to relax and recover from the excess adrenaline and steroid stress hormones that cause the stress response. Most important, the Meditation Page strengthens your daughter's abilities to keep thoughts she wants *in* her conscious mind and to keep unwanted thoughts *out* of her conscious mind. This can help your daughter maintain her focus on homework, tests, sports, or whatever she wants without being distracted. Learning this ability can help her keep angry, destructive, negative, unproductive, or any other unwanted thoughts from staying in her mind and interfering with other, productive thoughts. Meditation strengthens the ability to control thoughts just like weight lifting strengthens muscles.

What should I do with this exercise?

I encourage you to try this exercise a few times before teaching it to your child. If you cannot do it the first time, then try concentrating on the page for thirty seconds several times during the day until you can do it better. If you get interested in this exercise, I suggest that you try using the page to meditate every night for five or ten minutes. You may find the experience quite useful to calm your own mind. The more you practice, the more benefits you will notice.

My son cannot seem to do this. What's wrong?

It could be that your son is too young, or is not very motivated to learn this exercise. Try it a few more times. If that does not work, go back to the breathing or muscle-relaxation techniques.

I'm a teen interested in meditation to quiet my mind and relax. What do you have for me?

I print up my business cards to be used for relaxation meditation, and I have printed out a copy you can use on page 87. Carefully remove the Meditation Card Page from the book, paste it on card stock, and cut out the Meditation Card. Then you can carry it with you as a tool for relaxation and stress reduction everywhere you go. Here are the instructions:

> First, find the tiny spot that is formed where the two black lines cross and look only at that spot. Focus your mind on this tiny spot and direct all your thoughts into it. If you notice that your attention has started to wander, redirect it to the black spot. Whenever you notice that a stray thought has entered your head, just redirect your attention the spot. Then continue your focus.

As you continue to do this exercise, you will notice your body begin to relax and your thoughts become calmer and quieter. When you are finished,

THE MEDITATION CARD

Make a copy of the box below, paste it on card stock, and carry it with you to relieve stress.

Look at the two lines and notice the spot where the lines cross. When you can see this spot, focus your attention on it. Let every bit of your attention become focused on the spot. When a thought comes along to distract you, just redirect your attention to the spot and go on focusing.

The Bipolar Handbook for Children, Teens, and Families

WES BURGESS, M.D., PH.D.

you can use the your new calm and relaxed self to solve problems, interact with people, work on projects, or merely better enjoy your life. Carry the Meditation Card with you and use it before stressful classes, speeches, sports events, tests, or any other situations where you need focus and relief from stress. The card is so small that you can use it anywhere without being noticed. At home, keep the Meditation Card around to help you calm down and start your schoolwork, to refocus when you become distracted, and to relax before bedtime so you can get a restful night's sleep. You may want to make several of these cards so they will be around when you need them.

Can't I just learn to quiet my mind altogether? I want a break from my thoughts.

The big experts on quieting the mind are the successful practitioners of Zen meditation, which exists to teach people how to quiet their minds and stop thinking for a while. If this is what you need, contact someone locally who can teach you. If you cannot find anyone in your area, you may have to look in nearby communities.

Is this meditation stuff against the beliefs of my church?

The meditation techniques I am suggesting work to help heal your mind and give you better control over your thoughts. These exercises do not carry with them any sort of doctrine, and I know of no religious beliefs that they contradict. If you have any doubts, check with your own religious leader and show him or her the book.

I'm a modern teen and meditation isn't my style. Isn't there some other way I can help get control of my thoughts?

You can try thought-stopping techniques, such as the one that follows. Begin the process of monitoring your thoughts, so that you notice each time an intrusive, negative, or obsessive thought intrudes on your consciousness. This step alone will help bring you closer to controlling your thoughts. Then, when you notice an unwanted thought, lightly pinch the first knuckle of the first finger of your right hand and say or whisper, "I do not need to have this thought."

This behavioral routine serves several purposes. When performing these actions, you stop the thought in your mind, freeing up that space for desired, helpful thoughts. Also, repeating that you do not want the thought immediately after it occurs can help the unconscious part of your mind be prepared *before* the next intrusive thought to give you a better chance to filter it out before it even reaches your conscious mind. This approach can work very well for mild or moderately intrusive thoughts. However, if your thoughts are too hard to control, you may require medications to get them in order (see Chapter 5).

I have tried hard and I can't even begin to do any of these exercises without getting distracted. This is serious because unwanted thoughts interfere with my work in high school. Am I just out of luck?

These exercises are not easy when you first start to do them, but if you cannot begin to do any of them for even ten seconds, then you need to have your medications adjusted. You are far too prone to uncontrolled thoughts and this is something that mood stabilizers are good at fixing.

I have heard of other meditation techniques like visualizing what you want or imagining that you are in a pleasant place. Are these good for my bipolar child?

I don't agree with any exercise focusing on fantasies. One of the most important tasks in getting your child's mind back from bipolar disorder is to help him focus on the real, objective world around him and spend less time in fantasies. When your child purposely practices focusing on fantasies, it only makes it easier for bipolar disorder to control his mind. Similarly, if you concentrate on words or thoughts, even if they are nice ones, you are just exercising your ability to obsess about words or thoughts. In bipolar disorder, the goal is to be able to quiet the mind, turn thoughts on and off as desired, and increase awareness of the external reality all around us.

HEADACHES

Children suffering from bipolar disorder are more likely to have headaches than other children. Twenty-eight percent of bipolar children with migraines go on to have migraines as adults. Fortunately, some of the medications that treat bipolar disorder can also provide relief from headaches.

Are there lifestyle changes that will help my bipolar daughter's headaches?

I suggest that you start by eliminating stimulants like coffee, tea, and cola, cutting back on chocolate, and putting her meals, sleep, and exercise on a regular schedule. Keep track of the number and times of headaches and see if they correspond with any stressful events at school or at home. For example, are her headaches more frequent on Monday morning before she starts school or on Friday afternoon when she is especially tired? Do not get discouraged if the headaches go away and come back again. Headache treatment works by making headaches shorter and farther apart, but there will still be headaches now and then.

What are the first things you recommend when my daughter has a bad headache?

First, I would have her lie down in a dark quiet room with a cold cloth on her forehead. Sometimes just a little rest is all that is necessary. If your daughter can fall asleep, the headache will probably be gone by the time she wakes up.

If this is not enough, help your daughter concentrate on her breath or use the muscle-relaxation technique described on page 83 to relax, which will reduce her headache pain.

What's the single most important symptom to treat in severe migraines?

One of the worst symptoms of severe, debilitating headaches is nausea. It is often helpful to ask your doctor about an antinausea medication such as promethazine (Phenergan) or trimethobenzamide (Tigan). Try to get an agent in the form of a suppository, which can be given quickly if your bipolar child has a headache and feels sick to her stomach. Blocking nausea can often keep the migraine experience from becoming intolerable, if you act quickly enough.

What medication is taken most often for minor headache relief?

Almost all popular headache remedies contain one identical ingredient: caffeine. Although it is a good idea to avoid caffeine to prevent headaches, a burst of caffeine can sometimes help squelch them. The amount of caffeine in a standard bottle of caffeinated diet cola is usually about right for treating children's headaches. It is worth a try to see if your child responds.

My friends take medications for their migraines like Fiorinal, Fioricet, Medigesic, Esgic, and Sedapap. What are these and will they help my son's headaches?

These are old-fashioned barbiturate sedatives that are addictive and toxic. I never give them to anybody. Do not let anyone give them to your child.

What if my daughter's headaches continue?

Make sure your daughter's bipolar medicines are optimal. I have often seen headaches lessen or go away when bipolar symptoms stabilize on effective medications. If her headaches become too serious to handle at home, turn her headache problem over to your local doctor, neurologist, or headache specialist. The important thing is, do not get discouraged, and do not give up.

SUBSTANCE USE AND ABUSE

Teenaged alcohol and other drug abuse is a serious concern for parents of all children. However, bipolar disorder makes children ten times more likely to abuse substances than their schoolmates, and the risks are greater if drug use starts before eighteen years of age. Furthermore, most abused drugs can worsen your child's bipolar disorder.

Studies have shown that effective treatment of your child's bipolar disorder will reduce the risk of him or her becoming an alcohol or other drug abuser by 60 percent. I have known of instances where teens and young adults stopped using alcohol, cocaine, or other substances when their bipolar disorder came under good control. Many children have told me, "I just don't want it anymore."

Alcohol Abuse in Bipolar Children

Alcohol disturbs your child's brain function, working against his or her bipolar treatment and causing bipolar symptoms to get worse. It is as if your child spent all day cleaning the house and then let a herd of elephants run through. Some studies show that 50 percent of bipolar children will grow up with an alcohol or other drug abuse problem, so it is best to start early to help your child abstain from alcohol.

What should I tell my son to get him to stop drinking alcohol?

Tell your son that it is important for him to avoid drinking, for fear of worsening his bipolar illness. Tell him you realize he will be under a lot of pressure from television, movies, friends, and schoolmates to drink, but you are genuinely concerned about his health and his future and you do not want him to drink beer, wine, or mixed drinks.

My family has always consumed fine wine with dinner. Why must my daughter abstain from wine with her meal? It never troubled me as a child.

At present, I believe that it is too risky for bipolar children to be allowed to drink at all. Furthermore, you and your family may need to stop drinking to make sure your child does not learn habits that could ruin her life later.

My son asked me whether it was bad to drink while taking medications. What should I say?

If you look at the *Physicians' Desk Reference* (*PDR*) on the Internet or at the library (see Chapter 12), you will find a warning not to drink with any of the medications listed in this book. In addition to making bipolar disorder worse, drinking while taking medications can put an extra strain on the liver, making it easier to get liver problems. Tell him that it *is* bad to drink while taking medications.

I'm eighteen and live in an area where all the high school kids drink. Tell me, really, what is the maximum amount I can drink without worsening my bipolar disorder?

Really, you cannot drink at all without the possibility of worsening your bipolar disorder now and in the future. In my judgment, not even one drink is okay.

Will taking medications make my son more likely to be an alcoholic or a drug addict?

Current research shows that taking appropriate medications for bipolar disorder actually decreases your son's risk of alcohol and other drug abuse.

Stimulants

Stimulant medications abnormally increase the levels of adrenaline in the brain and body, worsening bipolar disorder. The general rule for bipolar disorder is "no stimulants."

I am an adolescent girl who enjoys her coffee. Is there any problem with that?

Caffeine is an addictive stimulant that increases adrenaline, causing insomnia, muscle tension, rapid pulse, sweating, and tremor. Although most people suffer no more than a mild shakiness, there are known cases where high doses of caffeine precipitated manic and psychotic episodes in individuals with bipolar disorder. Therefore, it is best to limit the consumption of coffee, tea, and energy drinks that contain caffeine to one per day.

What about cola? I drink several cans at school every day so I can get things done.

With few exceptions, soft drinks, bottled teas, and herb drinks contain high amounts of caffeine and other stimulants. Either stay away completely or limit your soft drink intake to just one 12-oz. caffeinated drink per day.

I drink only herbal teas and power drinks that don't list caffeine. Aren't those okay?

Herbs like guarana (*Pallinia cupana*) and yerba maté (*Ilex paraguariensis*) contain high levels of caffeine and related compounds. Manufacturers use them so they can make drinks caffeinated without actually listing caffeine on the label. Mallow (*Sida cordifolia*), bitter orange (*Citrus aurantium*), and several other herbal ingredients contain stimulating chemicals resembling adrenaline. Stay away.

I took Korean ginseng and I really got a lift. Is it okay to take it all the time?

Panax ginseng (Korean ginseng or red ginseng) is a plant that has a strong stimulant effect. I have seen cases where large doses of *Panax ginseng* triggered bipolar episodes so severe that hospitalization was necessary.

I heard that there are diet pills that would let me eat all I want, never exercise, and still lose weight.

I saw those same claims about mail-order pills on television and on the Internet last night. Sorry, Cinderella, but the ball is over. There is no magic way to lose weight. Moreover, nonprescription diet pills usually contain stimulants that can be dangerous for your heart and may make your bipolar disorder worse.

I am a bipolar teen with a weight problem. What about prescription stimulant diet pills?

Most prescription diet pills put a strain on your heart and can worsen your bipolar disorder. Examples include phentermine (Adipex or Ionamin), phendimetrazine (Bontril or Prelu-2), and benzphetamine (Didrex). These are potentially addictive and can cause anxiety, irritability, panic, paranoia, and psychosis. It is notable that generic drug manufacturers make phentermine in black, or black and yellow, capsules resembling "speed," so it can be sold as a street drug. Stay away.

A high school classmate tells me that SAMe makes her feel better. Can I take it?

SAMe (s-adenosyl-L-methionine) is naturally found in the body, where it affects brain adrenaline, serotonin, and dopamine, as well as many other body chemicals. Some studies suggest that it works like conventional anti-depressants in the brain. However, there are also reports of mania, anxiety, and insomnia triggered by SAMe. I advise you to avoid it for the present.

My son told me that *Salvia* is a natural, legal herb that makes other kids feels good. Is it okay?

I have seen *Salvia* trigger psychotic reactions in susceptible children. I do not think it will be legal for long. Tell your son to avoid it.

Q Can I smoke or not? My mother treats smoking like it is a drug addiction.

I have worked with many patients whose bipolar disorder became unstable when they smoked. Smoking reduces the amount of medicine that gets to your body, and some studies show that bipolar individuals who smoke have more than twice as high a rate of suicide than those who do not smoke. There are also cases on record where high doses of nicotine have triggered bipolar episodes. No smoking, please.

Q I heard that bipolar disorder is associated with heart disease. Is this true?

Currently, bipolar children have an increased lifetime risk for high blood pressure (35 percent) and high cholesterol (23 percent), with an increased likelihood of heart attack, heart failure, chronic obstructive pulmonary disease (COPD), and stroke. However, much of this risk comes from the large proportion of bipolar individuals who currently smoke cigarettes (40 percent). I fully expect that your child's risks will be less than this if he does not start smoking cigarettes as an adolescent.

Q I smoke marijuana, but only a puff or two a day. That's okay, right?

Marijuana is a drug with stimulant effects. It increases the activity of the adrenaline system, which can increase bipolar symptoms. Bipolar disorder can make you so sensitive to marijuana that you get high on just a puff. However, it is the effect on your body and brain that counts, not how much you need to take. I have known people who used marijuana who were *never* able to get their bipolar depression under control. Even a small amount can cause problems.

FIVE STEPS FOR REDUCING YOUR
CHILD'S BIPOLAR SYMPTOMS
WITH LIFESTYLE CHANGES

1. Encourage your child to go to bed and get up at the same times every day.
2. Encourage your child to eat proper meals at the same times every day.
3. Encourage your child to exercise hard every day, but not to overexercise.
4. Encourage your child to use relaxation techniques and meditation to reduce life stress.
5. Help your child avoid caffeine, cigarettes, alcohol, stimulants, and other substances that worsen bipolar disorder.

What is in common between cocaine and speed that worsens bipolar disorder?

Cocaine, methamphetamine (speed), and prescription drugs like bupropion (Wellbutrin, an antidepressant) and bromocriptine all increase the levels of a brain chemical called dopamine. This destabilizes bipolar disorder and can trigger bipolar depressive, manic, or psychotic episodes.

The counselor said my son was "self-medicating" by taking cocaine. Do you believe this?

There is nothing similar between your son taking appropriate bipolar prescription drugs, which make him feel like himself and make his brain work normally, and the use of cocaine, methamphetamine (speed), or other street drugs that make him feel high, make his brain work abnormally, and cause him to behave abnormally. Street drugs are no treatment for bipolar disorder, and their use is illegal drug abuse and not "self-medication."

5.

MEDICAL TREATMENT CAN HELP YOUR BIPOLAR CHILD

· ·

Parents usually approach medications with trepidation, and this is a good thing. Your primary responsibility is the health and welfare of your child, and whether your child receives medications is your choice to make. There are no guarantees that medications will work, and all medications have potential side effects. If you do not try medications, you will be safe in knowing that you did nothing to make things worse.

On the other hand, if you do choose to try medications, you will have offered your bipolar child the treatment that is most likely to stop bipolar disorder in its tracks and keep it from progressing as your child grows older. Of all the treatments available for bipolar disorder, medications are the most important for your child because only medications can make your child's brain and nervous system work the way they are supposed to. Best of all, medications may give you the wonderful opportunity to see your child the way he or she was meant to be without illness. Fortunately, the decision about giving your child medications is not quite as bad as it may appear. Learning what medications do and don't do, and learning what pharmacological treatment is all about, will help you guide your child and ease your nerves. If your child takes the right medication, you will be quickly reassured that it will not change your child's personality or rob your child of his or her specialness. For most parents, the first few weeks of seeing their child on medications lifts a heavy weight of fears and helps them relax in the understanding that their child *can* get better.

I'm terribly afraid of giving my daughter medications. Can you say anything to reassure me?

When you become part of the medical process yourself, through education and working closely with your daughter's psychiatrist, it will not seem so foreign or scary. As a parent, you have a special insight into your child's needs and nature that will guide your choices.

OK. Just make it very simple without any fancy doctor talk. What do medications do?

To make it simple and direct, medications replace chemicals that are missing from the brain. When brain chemicals are missing, the brain is unhealthy and cannot function. When the correct brain chemicals are provided, the brain can work the way it was supposed to, naturally.

Which medications are licensed to treat my child's bipolar disorder?

Almost none of the medications that have been used during the last forty years to treat bipolar disorder in children are licensed by the FDA for that purpose. Lithium salt is the only major bipolar disorder medication approved by the FDA and then only for treating adolescent mania. Many of the mood stabilizers, as you will see, are licensed for use in very young children for conditions other than bipolar disorder, but not for use in bipolar disorder. Even medications routinely used to treat bipolar disorder safely in adults and adolescents have not been licensed for use in children. There is a reluctance to do the clinical research necessary to obtain such licensure because of the legal liabilities any research institution would face trying unlicensed medications on sick children. These studies are very expensive and require extra review and permissions, and children are too variable in their response to be good research subjects. Pharmaceutical companies are quite happy to avoid the legal liability issue altogether by leaving their medications unlicensed with the assurance that doctors will continue to use them to treat their child patients with bipolar disorder. What this means is that, for now, we will get no help from the FDA or pharmaceutical corporations in treating our bipolar children.

If your child has been doing well on medications for years, this lack of support will not seem relevant. However, if you are just starting your child's medical treatment, you will have to find a physician who is knowledgeable and who you trust. This book can help you learn more about medications, and you can talk with other parents in your child's school and in parent support groups. Nevertheless, you will only have the reassurance you need when you see your child getting better and not developing any extra problems. Until then, education and a good relationship with your child's doctor are your mainstays in beginning your child's medical treatment.

Why does my bipolar daughter have to take medications? Isn't psychotherapy enough?

The right therapy with the right therapist is important for your daughter's recovery. However, medications must come first so that she can think clearly and participate actively in her therapy. Only medications can make her brain cells work normally. Medications are such a necessary part of bipolar treatment that in some situations it may constitute malpractice for a professional to recommend the use of psychotherapy alone. I have often said, "Psychotherapy *without* medicine produces one year's progress in five years; psychotherapy *with* medications produces five years' progress in one year."

How long will my son have to take medications for bipolar disorder?

Doctors are supposed to say that your son will have to take his same medicines forever, but I know that is untrue. Whatever your son is taking now, I am sure he will be receiving greatly improved treatments in the next few years. There is so much scientific work into the causes and treatment of

WHY CAN'T CHILDHOOD BIPOLAR DISORDER BE TREATED WITH PSYCHOTHERAPY ALONE?

1. Only medications can fix the dysfunctional bipolar brain cells at the heart of your child's bipolar disorder, which are causing your child to have problems controlling emotions and thoughts.
2. Only medications can stop unwanted, distracting thoughts and emotions from coming into your child's mind and driving out the positive, constructive thoughts and emotions that your child wants and needs.
3. It may be impossible for your child to learn in school when his or her attention, memory, and problem-solving abilities are impaired because of bipolar disorder.
4. Your child may not even be able to benefit from psychotherapy while focus, insight, and logic are impaired by bipolar disorder.

However, after medications have helped clear your child's mind and thinking processes, then great progress in all these areas is possible.

bipolar disorder and such a great push to find new medications and other treatments that your son will likely benefit from great treatment breakthroughs in the near future. So, the thing to do now is just be patient. If you are not completely happy with your son's bipolar medicines now, you can surely look forward to better treatments in the future. If you are completely satisfied now, then I am sure that you will be even more satisfied in the coming years.

I'd just like to delay my daughter's treatment as long as possible. Doesn't that seem reasonable to you?

Not really. As long as bipolar disorder remains untreated, your daughter cannot use her own talents, abilities, and intellect to the fullest. She will begin to think less of herself, and the resulting trail of unnecessary failures and disappointments will cause her to have lower expectations for her future. You run the danger that she will begin to believe that she is slow, unmotivated, and antisocial. Unfortunately, once children get used to the idea that they are not capable of being bright, creative, motivated, and self-sufficient, it is hard to change these beliefs.

But these problems will go away later if I finally give my son the medications, right?

Not necessarily. Bipolar disorder gets worse with age and with each bipolar episode. Unfortunately, this worsening is often permanent.

Is there any way I can stop my child's bipolar disorder from getting worse?

Currently, medications are the only things we know of that can block recurring bipolar symptoms and help keep the illness from getting worse.

How could medications possibly help my son's bipolar depression? It's caused by things like bad grades, bad friends, not getting along with his sister, and so forth.

Your son's depressive symptoms are most likely to come out when bad things happen and his stress level rises. However, no parent wants a child to be depressed, whether it is justified or not. Without depression, your child can be happier, get better grades, choose better friends, and get along better with his family members. Proper treatment will help your son solve his own problems and avoid further depressing events.

Why can't I just let my daughter develop at her own pace?

Of course we must let our children develop at their own most natural pace, but if your daughter is artificially delayed because of bipolar disorder, she may lose ground in development. Children are already forced to keep up a breakneck pace in school. If your daughter falls too far behind, she may not be able to catch up before she has to take entrance examinations or apply for college. Moreover, children who have trouble maturing socially end up with immature friends, bad influences, and a tendency to have troubled social lives. It is our job to try to remedy this situation before your daughter has lost too much time.

But my son is doing fine in school. Why should I worry whether he could be doing better?

It is important for your boy to have the self-satisfaction and joy that come with doing his best. Although your son is doing well now, he may be passing up an opportunity to be great if he cannot develop his natural talents and abilities to their fullest.

Why use medications when "natural" treatments are completely safe and have no side effects?

Currently there is no vitamin, herb, or supplement that will cause your bipolar child's dysfunctional brain cells to function the way they were designed to. No natural compounds have been found effective and safe for treating bipolar disorder, and some that are being offered to treat "depression" can make your child's bipolar disorder worse (see Chapter 4). Believe me, if there were more basic treatment options than medications you would be reading about them here.

Q Should we keep our daughter on the lowest dose that gives her any help, for safety's sake?

You should try to keep your daughter on the dose that provides *optimal* control of her bipolar symptoms. We want to give her the best treatment possible, and the benefits she receives from some drug treatments may correspond with higher doses.

Q Won't medications poison my son if he takes them for a long time? Don't they accumulate in his system?

I have heard this notion too, but I do not know where it originated. Most bipolar medicines leave your son's body in a few hours or a few days. Many

---

MEDICATIONS USED FOR BIPOLAR DISORDER

· · · · ·

Mood Stabilizers: The First Line of Treatment
- Proven mood stabilizers: carbamazepine, lithium, Depakote
- A newer mood stabilizer: Lamictal
- May have mood-stabilizing qualities: clonidine

Antipsychotics: The Second Line of Treatment
- Proven antipsychotics: Geodon, Seroquel, Zyprexa
- Older antipsychotics: trifluoperazine, Orap, and others

New and Unproven Treatments
- Nonpharmacological: repetitive transcranial magnetic stimulation (rTMS)
- New medications: antisteroids, glutamate regulators, new antiseizure medications

people have taken bipolar medications for decades, and their bodies show no evidence of accumulating anything. They usually take exactly the same dose of their medicine for years.

What's the deal with side effects from medications? Do you list them all?

No. I only have space to list some of the side effects that I know of for each medication. For all the details, you need to consult with your doctor and books like the *Physicians' Desk Reference* (*PDR*), listed in Chapter 12.

MOOD STABILIZERS

The category of medications called mood stabilizers is the foundation of bipolar treatment. Your bipolar child is not adequately treated unless he or she is taking a mood stabilizer medication. Mood stabilizers are a group of anticonvulsant medications that treat the dysfunctional brain cells causing your child's bipolar disorder. Mood stabilizers can normalize your child's extreme emotions of sadness, hopelessness, anxiety, fear, panic, irritability, and anger. Mood stabilizers can improve concentration; help keep out intrusive, unwanted thoughts; and decrease distractibility, all of which will improve your child's attention and school performance. My patients tell me that mood stabilizers remove the "fog" from their minds. Mood stabilizers also decrease impulsive behaviors that occur during periods of depression, anxiety, anger, or euphoria.

What do mood stabilizers do in my son's brain?

They stabilize brain cell membranes (sodium and calcium channels) to keep your son's brain cells firing at the normal rhythm. They also have other effects that calm your son's emotions and decrease the amount of steroid stress hormones.

Are there any mood stabilizers that can heal my child's brain cells?

There is some scientific evidence that carbamazepine, lithium salt, valproate, and lamotrigine can help protect and/or grow new, healthy brain cells. Some mood stabilizers, especially carbamazepine, are used after brain injury as part of the recovery process.

What symptoms of my daughter's bipolar disorder will mood stabilizers help?

Because they treat the dysfunctional brain cells that drive all bipolar symptoms, mood stabilizers will help all parts of your daughter's bipolar disorder.

Do mood stabilizers ever work miracles? I sure need one for my son.

I have seen dramatic turnarounds after giving carbamazepine, lithium salt, and valproate. However, different children and physicians may have different results.

Will mood stabilizers interfere with school or homework?

Actually, mood stabilizers should help your child do better schoolwork and homework, by increasing his attention, organization, memory, and ability to solve linear problems.

Will mood stabilizers take away my daughter's depression quickly?

Bipolar depression is not as easy to budge as unipolar depression. Moreover, bipolar depression causes the accumulation of poor sleep habits, poor social habits, and pessimistic attitudes, and it takes time for these habits to change. Bipolar depression treatment takes care and a little patience, but the effort will be worth it when your daughter's depressive symptoms begin to lift.

Will mood stabilizer medications help me play better baseball, soccer, or volleyball?

You need to think a lot to play these games. Child athletes playing these sports have told me that their performance improved after starting mood stabilizers, particularly in baseball. I think the improvements occur because these children are able to pay better attention, reason more quickly, and make more-logical decisions while playing on mood stabilizers. In addition to having better brainpower, players have also told me they were more coordinated, which I cannot explain. I have not noticed any particular advantage for the game of basketball.

My friend says her son took a mood stabilizer and his handwriting got better. Is this possible?

I have often seen bipolar children's messy, cramped handwriting improve after mood stabilizers were given.

What dosage will my son have to take and how is this decided?

Most doctors will start your son at a very low dose, just to be sure that he does not receive too much or have a bad reaction. Increasing the dose slowly allows his body to adjust to the medication and gives the doctor time to find the optimum dose.

How often will my son need to take his mood stabilizer medicine?

Your son needs to take his mood stabilizers every day at the same time. I recommend that he take his entire mood stabilizer dose at night. It is easier to remember that way and, if minor side effects occur, such as dizziness or blurry vision, they happen at night when he is asleep.

Will my son go back to the way he was if I take the mood stabilizers away?

Your son's bipolar thinking, emotions, sleeping problems, eating patterns, and fatigue will come back rapidly after his medications are withdrawn. The good habits that mood stabilizers helped your son build may last for weeks, but they too will fade away if the medication is discontinued.

Can I stop my daughter's mood stabilizers immediately?

Like all other medications, your daughter's mood stabilizer medications should be tapered slowly according to a doctor's instructions. Stopping them suddenly could potentially cause severe bipolar episodes or even seizures. Do not stop your daughter's mood stabilizer medications all at once.

WHY DOES THE DOCTOR TAKE BLOOD TESTS?

There are blood tests for carbamazepine, lithium salt, and valproate that will tell how much of the dose is available to the body. Here are some of the reasons blood tests are requested:

- To make sure your child is taking the medicine.
- To make sure your child is not taking too much medicine.
- To make sure that your child's blood, kidney, and liver functions are optimal.
- For use as a reference to compare with past and future blood tests.

How do blood tests help the doctor set the dose level for my son?

They don't. The doctor can only tell whether the dose is right by examining your son to see if he is better. You should also tell the doctor about your son's response to each new dose. The doctor will use your information and his or her examination to decide if a dose adjustment is warranted. Blood tests can tell us if the dose is too high, but they cannot tell us whether the dose is effective.

Why do all medications have two names?

The medication name in lower case is the generic name and the capitalized name is the brand name. I use mostly generic names but, because some people are more familiar with the brand names, I often list both.

Carbamazepine (Equetro, Carbatrol, Tegretol, Tegretol XR, and Other Brands)

Right now, carbamazepine is the mood stabilizer I prescribe the most. Carbamazepine is one of the three mood stabilizers that have been proven capable of stopping bipolar symptoms and keeping them from returning. Carbamazepine has been used in bipolar disorder for many years, and its effectiveness and safety are well understood. Of all the mood stabilizers around, my patients and their parents have the best things to say about carbamazepine. It is sold as Equetro, Carbatrol, Tegretol, and other brands, and it is available in time-release capsules, regular tablets, and chewable tablets. Carbamazepine is also available in a liquid form but, because it settles out in the bottle, I do not recommend it.

How is carbamazepine licensed?

Carbamazepine is licensed for use in adult bipolar disorder under the brand name Equetro. Tegretol, Carbatrol, and other forms of carbamazepine are licensed for use in children under six years of age for treating epilepsy, but not bipolar disorder.

How will my daughter feel when she takes carbamazepine?

Carbamazepine treats all of her possible bipolar symptoms, including anger, anxiety, attention, focus, hyperactivity, impulsive behaviors, intrusive thoughts, sleep problems, and difficulty with logic and analysis. Older children often say they feel more relaxed but, although their mood and school performance improve, younger children usually cannot tell that they are taking anything at all.

Can carbamazepine help my daughter with her bipolar depression?

I have received assurances from many of my patients and their parents that carbamazepine helps with their depressive symptoms.

I'm shy around the opposite sex. Will carbamazepine help that?

Carbamazepine is one of the medications I use to treat shyness and social anxiety in social anxiety disorder, and many bipolar children and adults find it helps with social anxiety born from bipolar disorder.

How long will my daughter have to wait for results after starting carbamazepine?

Unlike other kinds of medicines, you will be able to see positive results of carbamazepine within a few days of reaching your daughter's ideal dose. However, it may take several increases before the ideal dose is reached, especially if the doctor is being conservative.

What kinds of doses do you consider in carbamazepine?

I usually start with 100 mg to be taken at night and expect to begin to see a substantial effect around 400 to 800 mg. Many bipolar children need higher doses, but even 100 mg is enough to produce benefits in some. When starting carbamazepine, I often prefer to use the time-release formulas like Equetro, if the cost is not a problem. Ask your doctor for his or her own recommendations.

What are the minor side effects my son should expect from taking carbamazepine?

The most common side effects I have seen are dizziness, nausea, and fuzzy vision. Many children experience no side effects at all and, for others, only slight side effects occur that go away in a few days after starting the medication.

Q Does carbamazepine make you sleepy when you take it? I don't want to make my daughter feel sleepy.

Children often tell me that taking carbamazepine feels relaxing, and it may help children fall asleep at night. I suggest that your daughter take her car-bamazepine at bedtime, so that if she experiences any sleepiness it will oc-cur during the night and will be gone by morning.

Q Could my daughter get some really severe side effects from carbamazepine?

Like most medications, some rare severe side effects have been reported for carbamazepine. Your daughter could get a rash that usually consists of red-dish dots or blisters that spread from the middle of the chest outward and usually do not hurt or itch. If a rash occurs, her carbamazepine will have to be stopped right away or it could potentially cause sickness or even mortal-ity if left unchecked. However, I have seen fewer than a dozen cases of rash in all my years of practice, and all resolved quickly after the carbamazepine was stopped.

There have also been cases of anemia or insufficient blood cells that have been reported in people taking carbamazepine. These could be fatal if ignored. However, in my life history of using carbamazepine, I have never seen this anemia. One writer estimated the likelihood as one in a million. Ask your own doctor about his or her experience.

Q After my son takes carbamazepine for a while, will the doctor have to increase his dose?

The body makes its own enzymes to digest carbamazepine and this is why, after a few months' time, the level of carbamazepine in your son's blood-stream will naturally decrease. At this time, his doctor may wish to increase the dose slightly just to keep the level in his bloodstream the same.

How will the doctor monitor the amount of carbamazepine in my daughter's blood?

Blood tests can be taken to show the amount of carbamazepine in her bloodstream and to show the blood cell count to confirm that she does not have any anemia.

My sister takes carbamazepine for epilepsy. Is it the same as what's used in bipolar disorder?

In addition to bipolar disorder, carbamazepine is used in epilepsy, nerve pain, and other conditions.

Lithium Salt (Eskalith, Lithobid, and Other Brands)

The Greeks and Romans began a long tradition of sending nervous and manic individuals to spas to drink and soak in spring waters containing natural lithium salt. These calming springs continue to be used in Europe to this day. Unfortunately, your child would have to drink vast amounts of spring water to get enough lithium salt to improve his or her bipolar symptoms, and the amount of lithium your child consumed would vary from day to day. Therefore, lithium salt is now compounded in tablets and capsules that contain precise amounts of this natural substance.

Lithium salt was once one of the most popular over-the-counter medications sold in the United States. In its prescription form, lithium salt has been used to treat bipolar disorder in both children and adults for more than thirty years, and it has been proven to be effective in clinical studies and doctors' offices for more than a century.

How does lithium salt work in my daughter's body?

Lithium salt keeps your daughter's brain cells from being overreactive and makes her dysfunctional brain cells function normally. Lithium salt reduces dopamine and adrenaline, which can cause mania. Lithium salt also increases serotonin in the part of her brain that controls emotions (the limbic system), an effect that helps reduce her depression, anger, and suicidality. Lithium salt affects a brain chemical called inositol (see Chapter 4), which is another way lithium salt may be effective in bipolar disorder.

What's so good about lithium salt for my bipolar son?

Lithium salt works quickly, and is especially good at controlling anger, depression, and impulsivity. It also has a high likelihood of working in your child, and it is one of the three mood stabilizers that have been proven able to stop bipolar symptoms and keep them from coming back. I sometimes add a low dose of lithium salt to other bipolar medications to improve their effects in adolescents. Many older physicians are more comfortable and familiar with the use of lithium salt than with the use of other mood stabilizers because of its long clinical history. Lithium salt comes in a choice of regular capsules, time-release tablets, and a flavored liquid. Lithium salt is widely available and it is relatively inexpensive.

Is lithium salt licensed for treating bipolar disorder in children?

Lithium is the only drug with FDA approval for adolescent mania. It is licensed for the treatment of bipolar disorder from twelve years of age through adulthood. It is not licensed for use in young children, although it is frequently used for this purpose.

Will lithium salt help my daughter's depression?

One study showed that lithium salt significantly reduced depression in 80 percent of bipolar depressed individuals. This success rate is as good as or better than the effectiveness of antidepressants in the treatment of unipolar major depression. Because lithium is so effective, there is really no reason to consider giving antidepressants to bipolar depressed children.

Q Will lithium salt help keep my depressed child from suicidal thoughts?

Lithium salt has been shown in many studies to reduce suicidal thoughts and actions significantly. I think this is a reflection of how well lithium salt works overall in the treatment of bipolar disorder.

Q What is the difference between carbamazepine, valproate, and lamotrigine, which are called antiepileptic drugs (AEs), and lithium salt? Lithium salt seems to be the only mood stabilizer that doesn't help seizures.

Actually, there may not be as much difference as you might think. I have seen research indicating that lithium salt also has antiseizure properties at the right dose.

Q My son says he is thirsty and has to urinate after he takes his lithium salt. Why is that?

Taking lithium salt makes your son thirsty, just as using regular salt does. Consequently, he may drink more fluids and urinate more frequently. It is a good idea to avoid becoming dehydrated, but there is no need for him to drink fluid all the time, which could dilute medications and nutrients in the blood. Occasionally, a child prone to enuresis may wet the bed if he does not empty his bladder before bedtime.

Will the doctor want my daughter to take blood tests?

It is important to monitor levels of lithium salt in your daughter's blood to make sure she is not getting too much. Your doctor may also request other blood tests to check her kidney function and thyroid function.

What can happen if my daughter's lithium blood level goes too high?

If your daughter's lithium blood level is high, she may experience side effects like tremor and slurred speech. When the level of lithium salt is *very* high, it can harm her kidneys. Usually this is only a concern if your daughter becomes seriously dehydrated. This can happen if she is vomiting, sweating, having diarrhea, or experiencing a high fever during a period of illness. Always check with your doctor to see if you should lower or skip some of your daughter's lithium salt doses when she has the flu. It is a good idea to be aware of the blood test results and to keep your child hydrated, especially during the summer.

What should I do if my daughter has the flu and is losing fluids?

This is a good time to pay special attention to your bipolar child's fluid intake. There is an ideal product called Pedialyte that contains fluid and minerals for rehydrating children. Nowadays, you can find it in many grocery stores. It is a good idea to keep a bottle in your refrigerator at all times.

Will lithium salt affect my daughter's appearance?

Lithium salt makes it easier to gain weight, although the effect is not as strong as with valproate. Most of my patients taking lithium salt keep their weight under control nicely, but if a child is already overweight then another mood stabilizer might be better. On the other hand, lithium salt might help your daughter gain weight if she is too thin.

Lithium salt can also increase the occurrence of acne, an important fact to consider in appearance-conscious adolescents.

Would you really give my child lithium? I heard that's for crazy people.

Some people have the erroneous notion that lithium salt is only used in severe mental illness and that if you are taking lithium salt, then something terrible must be wrong. It used to be that, when an adult was extremely mentally ill, doctors would prescribe every medicine that might possibly help, and lithium salt was often part of the mixture. Perhaps this practice led to misconceptions about lithium salt.

What do you think of lithium salt?

I think that lithium salt is a good medication for bipolar disorder, especially if children are able to watch their weight effectively.

Valproate (Depakote, Depakote ER) and Valproic Acid (Depakene)

For years, valproate (Depakote) has been American doctors' favorite mood stabilizer. Much research has demonstrated that it is one of the best all-around drugs for adult bipolar disorder and it is one of the three mood stabilizers that have been proven to keep bipolar symptoms from returning in adults. However, I have not found it quite as useful as carbamazepine or lithium salt for the treatment of bipolar children because of its sedative qualities and other side effects.

Is Depakote licensed to treat bipolar disorder in children?

Depakote is licensed for treating bipolar disorder, but only in adults. It is also licensed for safe use for epilepsy in children from ten years of age, and it is licensed to treat migraine headaches in children sixteen years of age and older.

What symptoms of bipolar disorder will valproate improve?

As with other mood stabilizers, valproate treats the central cause of bipolar disorder, and it will improve most bipolar symptoms. My adult patients most frequently report more clarity of thinking and fewer obsessional thoughts.

In my experience, valproate seems to be less effective for treating bipolar depression than the other mood stabilizers, probably because it is more sedating, and both sedation and fatigue are important symptoms of bipolar depression.

What are some other problems with prescribing valproate to bipolar children?

Mild sedation is the chief complaint of my patients taking valproate. Also, of the three top mood stabilizers, valproate seems most likely to cause children to gain weight. Tremor in the hands or feet is also sometimes seen, which can interfere with physical performance and make children self-conscious.

There is clear evidence that valproate can worsen polycystic ovary disease in adult women by slightly raising male hormone levels. Unfortunately, we cannot predict which young girls will get polycystic ovary disease when they are older, or whether prior exposure to valproate will make this condition more severe in adulthood.

Are there any really serious side effects I should worry about with valproate?

Valproate occasionally increases the levels of liver function tests and, in rare cases, there are reports of valproate causing liver failure. Your doctor will help prevent this by taking blood tests periodically to confirm normal liver function. Also, when lamotrigine is given with valproate, it can push the valproate up to toxic levels.

What's the difference between Depakote and Depakene?

Depakote is valproate and related compounds in a coating that makes it easy on the stomach. In contrast, valproic acid (Depakene) is an uncoated compound that causes severe abdominal cramping. None of my patients has ever found it satisfactory. Oftentimes I have heard it said that Depakote and Depakene are equivalent, but they are not. My advice is, do not let anyone give your child Depakene.

In what forms does valproate come?

Depakote is available in regular and time-release tablets and lower-dose capsules that can be opened and sprinkled on food. The latter are convenient when starting a child on Depakote.

Lamotrigine (Lamictal)

Lamotrigine is the best-tolerated mood stabilizer. It is easy to take, produces few if any minor side effects when dosed properly, and does not require blood tests to gauge medication progress. It doesn't make children sleepy or gain weight. It comes in several sizes so children can take as few tablets as possible. Doctors are enthusiastic about lamotrigine and frequently prescribe it for children with bipolar depression. In many ways, lamotrigine seems like a perfect medicine.

Unfortunately, lamotrigine is not as powerful as the top three mood stabilizers even at the maximum recommended dose. I sometimes find myself tapering a child off lamotrigine to start them on carbamazepine, lithium salt, or valproate because the lamotrigine did not work. This is not easy because lamotrigine interacts with carbamazepine and valproate to change the amount of medications that reach the bloodstream, so many doctors may choose to start children on one of the other, stronger mood stabilizers first.

Isn't lamotrigine the only treatment for bipolar depression?

Right now lamotrigine is being marketed as the ideal treatment for bipolar depression. However, effective treatment with the other mood stabilizers also reduces bipolar depression symptoms. Lamotrigine has an advantage in treating bipolar depression because it is not at all sedating. Medications that have sedative properties can make bipolar children feel like they are depressed because sedation and fatigue are key components of bipolar depression.

What is lamotrigine licensed for?

Lamotrigine is licensed for treating bipolar depression in adults. Lamotrigine is licensed to treat epilepsy from two years of age through adulthood.

For which children do you usually prescribe lamotrigine?

I consider lamotrigine for children who cannot tolerate carbamazepine, litium salt, or valproate; for children who cannot tolerate blood tests; and for children who want to reduce the side effects of their current mood stabilizers.

What are the most common side effects my son might get from lamotrigine?

Actually, children experience few problems from taking lamotrigine. Even children who cannot tolerate any other medicine can usually take lamotrigine without complaints.

What are the worst possible side effects my daughter might expect from lamotrigine?

When lamotrigine was first released, there were occasional reports of a severe rash that seemed to be equivalent to the carbamazepine rash which, if allowed to go too far, could be potentially fatal. However, once doctors learned to increase lamotrigine very gradually, the number of cases of rash drastically declined.

How do you start lamotrigine?

It is easier to start lamotrigine than any other bipolar medication. It is available in regular and chewable tablets, and there is a standard dosing regime that advances the doses at a very slow pace. There is even a five-week starter pack available with all the pills arranged in order.

Are there any important drug interactions with lamotrigine?

Yes. If lamotrigine and valproate are given together, the valproate can increase lamotrigine blood levels until they are toxic. In contrast, lamotrigine decreases carbamazepine in the blood, so the addition of lamotrigine to carbamazepine can cause the emergence of bipolar symptoms. These effects persist for a while even after lamotrigine is stopped.

I'm lagging behind in school all day. Will lamotrigine give me energy?

Many children tell me that lamotrigine gives them extra energy. Certainly, lamotrigine will not make you drowsy, and if the fatigue associated with your depression is lifted, you should feel more energetic.

Q I am already overweight for my age range, and I can't afford to put on another pound. Does lamotrigine cause weight gain? Could I lose weight?

Lamotrigine does not seem to cause any weight gain. Some adolescents tell me they lose weight while taking lamotrigine, although whether this is because they feel more energetic and are more active, or because there is some mechanism within the drug itself that causes this effect, I do not know.

Oxcarbazepine (Trileptal)
Oxcarbazepine is a medication that resembles carbamazepine at the molecular level. I have found it helpful in treating adult bipolar disorder, but not as helpful as carbamazepine. If your child cannot tolerate blood tests, oxcarbazepine is another possible option.

Q How are the side effects with oxcarbazepine?

When oxcarbazepine came out, I had hoped that it would be as effective as carbamazepine, with fewer side effects. Unfortunately, some children experience side effects such as sedation, dizziness, and nausea, and a severe, potentially fatal rash has been reported.

Q Is oxcarbazepine licensed for treating bipolar disorder in children?

Oxcarbazepine is licensed for treating epilepsy in children four to sixteen years of age and in adults but it is not licensed to treat bipolar disorder.

Topiramate (Topamax)
Topiramate is another antiepilepsy medication, but its effectiveness in bipolar disorder is still under debate. Topamax is licensed to treat children under two years of age for epilepsy but it is not licensed for the treatment

of bipolar disorder at any age. At the present, topiramate's only use is as an add-on to more-effective mood stabilizers.

Topiramate has an energizing effect that can relieve depression and fatigue. Some physicians give topiramate with other mood stabilizers to prevent weight gain. I have had good success using topiramate to treat bipolar adolescent boys with rage episodes, aggression, and the inability to stay out of trouble at school. One of my patients says that her tendency to go on shopping sprees and spend money impulsively only stopped when we added topiramate to her other bipolar medications. I have also known some specialists who used topiramate in the treatment of the migraine headaches that often occur in bipolar children.

I read on the Internet that Topamax scrambles your brain. That seems pretty objectionable.

I have read the same things. However, my patients have reported few thinking problems at reasonable doses. This may be because I start with low doses, and I usually limit the maximum doses I prescribe to between 50 and 150 mg daily.

Does Topamax have any other serious side effects my son should worry about?

Among other things, topiramate can sometimes decrease the amount of natural bicarbonate ions in the bloodstream. This can produce an imbalance in the acidity of the blood and fluid around the brain. However, none of my patients has ever had this side effect.

I need to lose weight. I'd take topiramate or anything if I might lose weight. Will I?

Many of my bipolar patients have lost unnecessary weight while taking low to moderate doses of topiramate.

SOME ANTISEIZURE MEDICATIONS
MAY NOT WORK WELL

Although all mood stabilizers are somewhat effective at treating temporal seizures, not all antiseizure medications are good for treating bipolar disorder. You need to know about these medications in case a doctor offers to give them to your child.

Gabapentin (Neurontin)

You can be sure that, sometime, some doctor is going to offer to give your bipolar child gabapentin. Gabapentin produces few side effects, has few medication interactions, and produces a feeling of mild relaxation that is pleasing to most people. These properties have induced doctors to try it for bipolar disorder, chronic pain, nerve injury pain, migraine headaches, panic, anxiety, and many other conditions.

Despite its lack of problems, gabapentin is not a good mood stabilizer. I have never seen bipolar disorder completely relieved by gabapentin, and there is no evidence that it can block the onset of bipolar episodes. Even at doses eight to ten times greater than usual, gabapentin is of no use as a solo treatment for your bipolar child. There are a few reports that gabapentin caused unstable emotions, poor concentration, and hyperactivity in children.

Although it is not licensed for this purpose, your child *might* get some benefit from gabapentin if it is added to other mood stabilizers.

Pregabalin (Lyrica)

Pregabalin is a variant of gabapentin that is licensed for the treatment of temporal lobe epilepsy and nerve pain associated with diabetes and shingles. Pregabalin is not licensed to treat bipolar disorder in children or adults, although its patent (U.S. Patent 6,359,005) lists bipolar disorder as one of its intended uses.

Pregabalin can cause dizziness, sleepiness, and blurred vision, as well as swollen hands and feet, weight gain, and impaired concentration. Pregabalin is already being promoted for a variety of mental and emotional disorders, but evidence that it is helpful in bipolar disorder is lacking.

Levetiracetam (Keppra)

Levetiracetam is licensed for treating epilepsy in children four years old through adulthood. It is not licensed for bipolar disorder at any age. Levetiracetam is known to cause sleepiness, muscle weakness, depression, and psychosis. The occurrence of violent anger and aggression has already been given the nickname "Keppra rage." I have not yet met any parents who were enthusiastic about levetiracetam for their children's bipolar disorder. I am currently waiting for more information on effectiveness and safety before I use levetiracetam in children. This drug should never be used in conjunction with carbamazepine, as it may cause toxicity.

Tiagabine (Gabitril)

Although many bipolar individuals have received it, there are no studies that show that Tiagabine is any help whatsoever for bipolar disorder. By contrast, there are many reports of tiagabine inducing serious seizures (called nonconvulsive status epilepticus) in patients who have never had any seizures before, including patients with bipolar disorder. Tiagabine is not licensed for use in bipolar disorder, and tiagabine can produce undesirable side effects like sleepiness and a feeling of drunkenness. I do not recommend tiagabine for your bipolar child.

Zonisamide (Zonagran)

Zonisamide is only licensed for the treatment of epilepsy in adults. It can cause a serious drug reaction if your child is allergic to sulfa drugs. It can also cause a severe skin rash, anemia, difficulty concentrating, drowsiness, dizziness, and nausea. I am not using zonisamide to treat children at this time.

ANTIPSYCHOTICS

Antipsychotics were one of the first psychiatric medications, and they have been in use for many years. Initially, they were only used at relatively high doses to treat psychotic mental illness. However, twenty years ago, the wise old white-haired doctors told me that "a tiny bit of antipsychotic added to mood stabilizer medicine is very helpful for bipolar disorder." Now that newer, safer medications called atypical antipsychotics are available, low doses of these medications are again being used to treat bipolar disorder. New research studies show that antipsychotics can help children regain control of their thoughts, reduce impulsive behaviors, reduce tantrums, and decrease rigid, compulsive behavior. They help regain healthy sleep patterns, and some antipsychotics can even help depressed children regain their motivation. Although the original antipsychotic medicines could cause serious movement disorders, the most commonly discussed side effect of the new atypical antipsychotics is weight gain.

Atypical antipsychotics offer many benefits for bipolar children. Children generally tolerate them well, especially at low doses. Unlike the major mood stabilizers, they do not require children to get regular blood tests to chart their progress. Nevertheless, do not enter this class of medications lightly. Many antipsychotics are licensed for bipolar disorder but none is licensed for use in children. Also, there is little research studying the effects of antipsychotics on children. Antipsychotics should only be considered after children have been optimally treated with mood stabilizers, or if they are showing psychotic behavior (see Chapter 11). Many doctors consider adding low-dose antipsychotics after children have been stabilized on mood stabilizers, in hopes of improving the overall treatment. Be aware that adding an antipsychotic to a mood stabilizer can potentially lower the effect of the mood stabilizer, so careful choice and adjustment are necessary.

Why do these medications work in bipolar disorder?

Antipsychotics decrease a neurotransmitter chemical called dopamine, which can trigger bipolar episodes or even psychosis when there is too much of it. In addition to the dopamine connection, these medications have a variety of other effects on serotonin, adrenaline, and other brain chemicals. For example, some act on certain adrenaline receptors (called alpha 1a) to control the flow of adrenaline to the brain.

Why not use antipsychotics instead of mood stabilizers in my son?

Unfortunately, antipsychotics work differently than mood stabilizers and probably do not reach all the dysfunctional brain cells that cause bipolar disorder in your son. This means that they can treat some of his symptoms but not others, and you cannot be sure that they will block new episodes from occurring.

Aren't antipsychotics used to treat schizophrenia?

That's true, but they are prescribed at much higher doses for schizophrenia than the doses needed for treating bipolar disorder, and I think antipsychotics have different effects at those higher doses.

What's the worst side effect that could happen with antipsychotics?

Before atypical antipsychotics, there was much concern about the risk of tremor, hyperactivity, muscle spasm, slowed movement, and other movement disorders that were not always reversible. Much of this concern about movement disorders has waned since the development of atypical antipsychotics.

I read about an atypical antipsychotic called Geodon. How can it help bipolar disorder?

I prescribe more ziprasidone (Geodon) than any other antipsychotic at this time. Low-dose ziprasidone is especially good for symptoms of depression and anger. Of all the atypicals, low-dose ziprasidone is the least likely to cause sleepiness or weight gain. It usually does not increase blood cholesterol, or produce interactions with other drugs, especially if it is taken with carbamazepine.

What doses of ziprasidone do you prefer?

I have heard other clinicians tell me that their bipolar patients have become agitated at low doses, so they try to increase the dose quickly. However, my patients have not reported this side effect, perhaps because I recommend especially low doses like 10 to 40 mg daily.

I read that Zyprexa is the best medication for bipolar disorder. Would it be best for my child?

Olanzapine (Zyprexa) is probably more effective for bipolar disorder than all the other popular atypical antipsychotics. Unfortunately, it is sedating, and it requires hard work by patients to keep from gaining a lot of weight. Weight gain can produce diabetes, and doctors are now very concerned about diabetes when prescribing olanzapine. I do not recommend giving olanzapine to anyone who already has a weight problem. Valproate and olanzapine are a particularly bad combination because both contribute significantly to weight gain.

Another mother told me about Seroquel. What can it add to my bipolar child's treatment?

Quetiapine (Seroquel) is an atypical frequently used in the treatment of bipolar disorder. It can cause minor weight gain, and it makes patients feel sleepy, so it is good to take at night as long as the sedative effects do not extend to the daytime.

Overall, I find quetiapine less useful than ziprasidone or olanzapine, and I am sometimes limited in the dose I can give because of its sedative effects. However, it may be a good choice if children are having insomnia at night or agitation during the day.

What sort of Seroquel doses are best?

There is no good evidence that doses higher than 600 mg daily are any more effective than lower doses.

My neighbor's child is taking Risperdal. What about that?

Risperdal (risperidone) was one of the first atypical antipsychotics. I have not seen success with Risperdal in bipolar children. I have repeatedly seen individuals who came to me on risperidone stabilize when they were taken off.

Do you use a lot of Abilify (aripiprazole)?

Aripiprazole is a newer atypical antipsychotic. Research to date indicates that nausea, constipation, and urinary incontinence are potential side effects. I am still waiting to see more research studies before I consider aripiprazole for children.

I heard people talk about Clozaril as if it was a miracle drug. What's that about?

There is a very powerful and effective atypical called clozapine (Clozaril). Unfortunately, it is plagued by severe side effects, requires frequent blood tests, and puts on weight like peanut butter. I usually avoid using clozapine in children.

What other antipsychotics have been used in bipolar disorder?

Years before the availability of atypicals, many doctors used trifluoperazine (Stelazine) at the lowest doses for bipolar disorder. In general, it did not make patients sleepy or gain weight. Some adult patients have told me that they felt their bipolar disorder was better controlled with trifluoperazine than with olanzapine. Although I have never seen them in my patients, trifluoperazine has the potential to cause all the movement side effects described above, so ask your doctor about its use.

What is the lowest dose of an antipsychotic you can give?

In the past, I have used an older antipsychotic called pimozide (Orap) at extremely low doses. It takes 2¼ days for half a pimozide tablet to leave the body, so 1 mg can be given every two to three days. Pimozide is so strong that I have often seen significant increases in motivation with doses this low.

However, pimozide is an older antipsychotic with the potential for the movement side effects that I have described above, as well as the possibility of triggering heart irregularity, at least at higher doses. Your child's doctor should be able to help evaluate this drug's potential benefits and side effects.

BLOOD PRESSURE MEDICATIONS CAN BE USED FOR BIPOLAR DISORDER

It seems odd that medications used to control high blood pressure should also be useful in the control of bipolar disorder. However, high adrenaline is an important factor in causing high blood pressure in adults. Because of this, medications that control adrenaline have been developed to treat blood pressure, and these are also available for use in controlling the adrenaline response in individuals with bipolar disorder. Surprisingly, I have rarely seen these medications lower blood pressure significantly in bipolar individuals, unless they had high blood pressure to begin with.

I have talked with other physicians who consider these blood pressure medicines safer than mood stabilizers or antipsychotics. However, you should note that none of these medicines is licensed for treating bipolar disorder in children or adults.

Clonidine (Catapres)

Clonidine is marketed, sold, and licensed only as an adult blood pressure medicine. However, it is widely used as a treatment for Tourette's disorder and ADHD in children and it has mood-stabilizing effects. It also is effective in reducing intrusive thoughts. In addition to tiny, easily swallowed tablets, clonidine also comes in state-of-the-art Catapres TTS patches. These patches look like Band-Aids, dispense medication directly through the skin, and need to be changed only once a week.

How could clonidine be helpful for my son's bipolar disorder?

Clonidine has mood-stabilizing effects. It can regulate adrenaline levels in your son's body and brain, thus providing him with some additional protection from stress. Clonidine works quickly, and I can often taper up to the optimum dose in a month's time or less.

Moreover, of all the medicines used in bipolar disorder, clonidine is one of the best for sleep. It is often possible to find a dose of clonidine that will allow your child to get to sleep and stay asleep during the night, without daytime hangover. Once you find the correct dose, it may continue to help sleep for years without any need to increase the dose.

In addition, some specialists find clonidine useful in the treatment of childhood migraine headaches, although it is not licensed for this purpose.

Would clonidine help my girl's school performance?

Clonidine can decrease your daughter's distractibility and her intrusive thoughts, which is important for success in schoolwork. Clonidine is the only medication for which a bipolar child has told me, "It makes my boring classes more interesting."

In what doses can my son take clonidine?

Clonidine pills and Catapres TTS patches are available in 0.1 mg, 0.2 mg, and 0.3 mg strengths, which are usually the only doses I prescribe.

I have never heard of clonidine. How good could it be?

I have had success in reducing bipolar symptoms with clonidine in the most severe cases of bipolar disorder imaginable. These were individuals reduced to living under highway underpasses and in doorways. Even under such horrible conditions, I was surprised at how much clonidine helped. Often clonidine can be used to start treatment and in some, clonidine may be sufficient to treat mild symptoms. Overall, patients and parents like clonidine better than any other medication I offer. Nevertheless, it is not licensed for use in childhood bipolar disorder, and you must have a good connection with your physician to oversee and follow up clonidine treatment.

Clonidine is a blood pressure medicine but my daughter's blood pressure is fine. What's up?

I have never seen clonidine lower blood pressure in children who had normal blood pressure, but it is still possible, so blood pressure should be monitored anyway. There are cases of blood pressure rising when clonidine was withdrawn suddenly, so, like all medications, clonidine should be discontinued slowly under a doctor's supervision.

Are there any other alternatives to clonidine?

Clonidine belongs to a class of medications called alpha-agonists. Other medications have similar effects, including guanfacine (Tenex) and guanabenz (Wytensin), but I do not use them.

Propranolol (Inderal)

Propranolol is another blood pressure medicine that can calm the physical response to stress. It is only licensed to treat adult blood pressure, but it is used for many conditions. For example, I frequently prescribe propranolol to actors and speechmakers in order to quiet their performance anxiety and eliminate stage fright. A large proportion of the actors you see on television and in films are taking propranolol. In addition, propranolol is useful in the treatment of migraine headaches, a problem that bipolar children frequently face.

Overall, propranolol is useful for temporary stress reduction but I do not give it on a regular basis. It has potential side effects, so work closely with your doctor if you want your child to try it.

Calcium Channel Blockers

There is a family of medications called calcium channel blockers that includes verapamil (Calan), diltiazem (Cardizem), and nifedipine (Procardia).

These medications work by changing the way electrical charges pass through nerve cells. They are licensed for use in high blood pressure, heart problems, and headaches, including migraines. Calcium channel blockers also have some mood-stabilizing properties. I have used them to supplement major mood stabilizers when other medications were not effective or could not be tolerated. Calcium channel blockers are not licensed for bipolar disorder and they each have their own side effects, so make sure that your doctor educates you about these medications before trying them.

SEDATIVE MEDICATIONS

Antianxiety medicines like diazepam (Valium), alprazolam (Xanax), clonazepam (Klonopin), lorazepam (Ativan), and Oxazepam (Serax), as well as sleeping pills like triazolam (Halcion) and zolpidem (Ambien), are simple sedatives. At low doses they are relaxing, at medium doses they put you to sleep, and at high doses they cause anesthesia. If the dose is too high, you stop breathing. These medications do not target dysfunctional brain cells. Instead, they just make users less aware of their thoughts and emotions. None of them is licensed for bipolar disorder. They are all potentially addictive, and are dangerous in overdose. Individuals who take antianxiety medications daily have more colds and infections. These sedatives can disinhibit children, causing increased anger and depression, and they can interfere with children's memory and learning processes. I try to avoid using these medications in children.

When used for sleep, sedatives make children unconscious at night, but they interfere with natural sleep rhythms and normal restful sleep. To improve bipolar children's sleep, I first focus on optimizing their bipolar medicines and then use the relaxation techniques described in Chapter 4.

Why are my child's friends being given sedatives?

Sedatives are an easy way to calm children down during the day and put them to sleep at night. I do not agree with this use.

Do sleep medicines ever cause hallucinations?

Yes. Several of my adult patients have experienced serious psychotic episodes while taking sedatives including triazolam (Halcion) and zolpidem (Ambien), which are also quite addictive.

FUTURE TREATMENTS FOR
BIPOLAR DISORDER

There is a tremendous effort now to find new treatments for bipolar disorder, including medications that work in new ways and medical treatments that do not use drugs.

So what are some of these new medications?

Some of the medications that might help bipolar disorder include antalarmin (A8727), ketoconazole (Nizoral), aminoglutethimide (Cytadren), and metyrapone (Metopirone), which decrease the production of steroid stress hormones. Memantine (Namenda) regulates glutamate (GLU), which also helps reduce the body's production of steroid stress hormones. Meridia (Provigil) increases histamine and choline, and is being tried in adults for treating the fatigue of bipolar depression. Triptorelin (Trelstar) reduces male hormone levels and may be helpful in reducing obsessive, aggressive, and hypersexual problems in boys.

I hope that some or all of these medications will soon be proven safe and effective for treating bipolar disorder in children. However, I am awaiting the results of ongoing research before recommending them at this time.

I heard that stimulating the brain with magnets relieved depression. Could my daughter use them?

There is a procedure called repetitive transcranial magnetic stimulation (rTMS), in which a strong magnetic field is passed through a magnet placed against the subject's head. It is not licensed in the United States, but I get calls every week from colleagues in Canada and other countries offering to perform rTMS on my patients. Preliminary tests are encouraging, but many current studies use unstandardized measures, lump together bipolar and unipolar depression, or are otherwise inadequate. Currently, we have no good evidence that rTMS would be safe for your daughter. It might even cause mania or increase her depression. There are ongoing clinical studies of rTMS for bipolar disorder at major universities. After these studies are published, I will have more to say on the subject.

What is vagal nerve stimulation and how could it help my bipolar daughter?

Vagal nerve stimulation, or VNS, is a technique in which a pacemaker is surgically implanted and used to stimulate nerves in the patient's chest. VNS has been shown to decrease seizures and improve depression in cases so severe that nothing else helps. This surgical procedure is extreme compared to medications and therapy, and I have preliminary information that VNS triggers manic symptoms. Therefore, I am not recommending it at this time.

So what should I know about these new treatments?

If we are patient we will benefit from great advances that are going to be made in the treatment of our children. If your child's condition becomes so bad that available treatments do not help, there are still some other options.

SOME MEDICINES CAN MAKE YOUR CHILD'S BIPOLAR DISORDER WORSE

Just as there are medications that provide the correct chemical balance for your child's brain, there are others that can upset this balance and worsen bipolar disorder. The FDA does not specifically test the safety of medications in children with bipolar disorder, so many medications available by prescription and in the drugstore can make bipolar children sick. In particular, medications that elevate the brain chemicals adrenaline and dopamine can provoke bipolar mania, depression, or even psychosis. After working so hard with your child to make his bipolar disorder better, you would not want him to take anything that would make his bipolar disorder worse.

Antidepressants

In my opinion, antidepressants should *never* be given to children with bipolar depression. Antidepressants are made for the treatment of unipolar major depression, which is a different disease than bipolar disorder, located in a different part of the brain and involving different brain chemicals.

Controlling bipolar disorder depends on *reducing* adrenaline, dopamine, and steroid stress hormones by stabilizing bipolar brain cells. Antidepressants work in the reverse by *increasing* brain adrenaline, dopamine, and serotonin, which makes bipolar symptoms worse. Antidepressants can cause bipolar mania, increased depression, or psychosis in children with bipolar depression. Furthermore, antidepressants often provide no help for bipolar depression in children anyway.

WHAT PROBLEMS COULD ANTIDEPRESSANTS CAUSE IN MY BIPOLAR CHILD?

. . . . . .

1. Antidepressants may not help your child's bipolar depression at all.
2. Antidepressants may seem to work at first, but then stop working.
3. Antidepressants may impair your child's everyday thinking and cause anxiety, agitation, and insomnia.
4. Antidepressants can worsen your child's bipolar depression.
5. Antidepressants can cause your child to have a severe manic episode, even if your child has never experienced mania before.
6. Antidepressants can cause your child to become psychotic and experience disorganized thoughts, delusions, and hallucinations.
7. Antidepressants can cause irreversible changes in your child's brain that make it easier to develop severe bipolar episodes now, and that make your child's bipolar disorder more severe and harder to treat for the rest of his or her life.

Take a look at Dr. Bryan Roth's PDSP Database Web site, listed in Chapter 12, to find out exactly which brain chemicals are stimulated by each antidepressant.

Q I read that studies show that giving antidepressants to people with bipolar disorder isn't as bad as you say. Some studies found that only 20 percent of adults developed bipolar manic episodes with antidepressants.

Twenty percent of patients developing mania is a terrible disaster. That means one in five adults given antidepressants experiences a mental breakdown, potentially forfeiting everything they have worked so hard to get in their life. I do not like those odds.

Moreover, such reports usually do not list the percentage of people whose depression increased, who had psychotic episodes, whose symptoms worsened after the end of the study, or whose bipolar disorder became permanently more severe and resistant to treatment for the rest of their lifetimes. In fact, the potential cost of worsening bipolar disorder is so great that we should only prescribe medicines that *decrease* the risk of bipolar episodes.

Q But aren't antidepressants safe for my bipolar son if they are given with a mood stabilizer?

I wouldn't count on it. Several studies indicate that antidepressants are just about as likely to cause mania in children whether they are given with a mood stabilizer or alone. Even if giving antidepressants with a mood stabilizer does not cause problems right away, antidepressants could still cause irreversible changes in your son's brain that make his bipolar disorder worsen over time. We should never do anything that might make a child's bipolar disorder worse, especially if the effect might be permanent.

Q **Are the pharmaceutical companies aware of this problem?**

Pharmaceutical companies are very aggressive about pursuing mood stabilizers and antipsychotics that can relieve the symptoms of bipolar depression, but I think they are still worried that they will lose money if they advise doctors and the public not to give depressed children antidepressants.

Q **Why has the rate of severe, treatment-resistant bipolar disorder risen in the last ten years?**

No one knows exactly. However, many of us believe that the frequency and severity of bipolar disorder have increased because bipolar depressed children have been given antidepressants. This single mistake may be responsible for incalculable unnecessary suffering. It is a trend I hope can be reversed.

Q **I read about children who shot their schoolmates after taking antidepressants. What caused this?**

No one can say for sure, but I wonder if children who commit violent acts after being given an antidepressant are really misdiagnosed bipolar children having a psychotic episode caused by the antidepressant they received.

Q **My bipolar niece says she can't stop her antidepressants or her symptoms come back.**

Withdrawing antidepressants creates a slight withdrawal, which sometimes causes increased depression, mania, and/or worsening of bipolar symptoms.

Consequently, the rule is that if a child is already on an antidepressant, first try to provide the maximum support with mood stabilizers, and then withdraw the antidepressant very slowly.

What antidepressants have you seen trigger mania or worsen bipolar depression?

I have seen the following antidepressants worsen bipolar disorder in children or adults: fluoxetine (Prozac), citalopram (Celexa), fluvoxamine (Luvox), bupropion (Wellbutrin), desipramine (Norpramin), escitalopram (Lexapro), imipramine (Tofranil), protriptyline (Vivactil), amitriptyline (Elavil), and phenelzine (Nardil). At high doses, I have seen mania triggered by paroxetine (Paxil), sertraline (Zoloft), and doxepin (Sinequan).

Is there any medicine sold as an antidepressant that does not worsen bipolar disorder?

I would never recommend that a bipolar child take an antidepressant. However, I have never seen low doses of trazodone (Desyrel) worsen bipolar disorder.

My aunt works for the drug company that makes Symbyax. Is it any good?

Symbyax is a combination of that company's most popular antidepressant, fluoxetine (Prozac), and its top-selling antipsychotic, olanzapine (Zyprexa), in one pill. Unfortunately, Symbyax contains none of the major mood stabilizers that are the cornerstone of bipolar treatment. Some studies indicate that Symbyax provides no protection from the onset of new bipolar episodes. In addition, we know that antidepressants like Prozac can trigger mania, deepen depression, cause psychosis, and make bipolar illness permanently worse.

What are MAOIs? Would they help my bipolar daughter?

Monoamine oxidase inhibitors (MAOIs) were the first medications that were found to reduce depression, anxiety, anger episodes, and other emotional disorders. Unfortunately, when MAOIs are taken with certain drugs and foods they can cause an increase in blood pressure that can be fatal. Therefore, I do not use MAOIs in children.

What about EMSAM? They say it's an MAOI that doesn't cause side effects.

Selegiline (also called deprenyl, Eldepryl, and EMSAM) is a type of MAOI that does not cause the potentially fatal blood pressure effect when used at low doses. EMSAM is selegiline in the form of a patch that can be applied to the skin.

Unfortunately, I have seen selegiline trigger mania on numerous occasions. Some experts have suggested that this is caused by methamphetamine (speed), which is produced when EMSAM is broken down in the body. As one young bipolar depression sufferer told me, "Before I took selegiline, I slept all the time. Now I never sleep."

PAIN RELIEVERS

What's the safest thing to give my bipolar teen for inflammation and pain?

The safest thing you can give older children for pain is probably acetaminophen (Tylenol). Aspirin, ibuprofen (Motrin, Advil), and similar medications have anti-inflammatory action that may be useful in older children with injuries. Consult your pediatrician and/or family doctor for his or her recommendations for young children.

Q Is there any danger to my bipolar son if
I keep minor pain medications
around my house?

If your son became depressed and took a regular bottle of extra-strength acetaminophen (Tylenol) or a king-size bottle of regular acetaminophen, it might be enough to cause him serious harm or death. Do not keep this much medication around your house.

Q Do drugstore pain relievers contain extra
ingredients that might worsen my girl's
bipolar disorder?

Drugstore combination products often contain decongestants and caffeine that stimulate the adrenaline system and may destabilize your daughter's bipolar disorder. As a general rule, do not buy combination cold or allergy products and always check with your psychiatrist before giving your daughter any new medicine.

Q Can narcotic prescription pain medicines
make my child's bipolar disorder worse?

I try never to give any narcotics to bipolar children. Narcotics can worsen bipolar disorder, make bipolar depression worse, cause mania, or even trigger psychosis. I have seen hydrocodone (Vicodin, Hycodan, Lorcet, Norco), oxycodone (OxyContin, Percodan, Tylox), and propoxyphene (Darvocet, Darvon) all worsen bipolar symptoms. Narcotics are also quite addictive, with Vicodin at the top of the list, so never let a dentist or other doctor give your child any of these narcotics. Injections of meperidine (Demerol) are frequently given in hospital emergency rooms for pain. I have seen many bipolar episodes triggered by meperidine.

Why does my daughter's bipolar disorder get worse when she goes to the dentist?

When dentists inject your daughter with anesthetics like procaine (Novocain), lidocaine (Xylocaine), or mepivacaine (Carbocaine), they have two choices. They can give the analgesic with or without adrenaline, which they refer to as "EPI" (pronounced "epp'-ee"). The EPI (adrenaline) is included in the injectable painkillers to decrease bleeding from tiny blood vessels. However, it can also destabilize your daughter's bipolar disorder, so always tell your dentist, "No epp'-ee!" Tell the emergency room doctor the same thing if your bipolar child needs an injection of local anesthetic to get stitches after an injury.

What about general anesthetic for controlling pain during surgery?

If your child has to have surgery, you must tell the surgeon and anesthesiologist all the medications your child is taking and follow their advice to avoid drug interactions. I have seen some bipolar children experience problems after receiving general anesthetics, and I am currently working on recommendations for the best types to use.

Are there any treatments for pain that don't involve taking medicine?

Yes. Relaxation techniques, meditation, guided imagery, ice, and rest all help reduce the effects of pain. There is also a technique that involves applying low-level electrical stimulation to the skin over the areas of skin innervation called TENS. This can be remarkably helpful if you can find an experienced practitioner.

COUGH, COLD, AND ALLERGY MEDICINES

In general, over-the-counter (OTC) drugs that you can buy at your drug-store without prescription have never been tested on bipolar children. Some of them can destabilize your child's bipolar disorder, and others may trigger bipolar depression, mania, or psychosis.

Are all cough medicines okay for my bipolar daughter?

Twelve-hour syrups and lozenges obtained over-the-counter from the drug-store usually contain a narcotic called dextromethorphan. I have seen it produce mania and psychosis in adults with bipolar disorder, and it should be avoided. Four-hour cough medicines without decongestants do not seem to cause problems for bipolar children, but they do not work very well either.

What can I use for my daughter's coughing? She's sick and her cough is terrible.

Diphenhydramine syrup (Benadryl elixir) reduces the cough impulse and provides a cooling, anesthetic feeling in the throat. Phenol throat spray (Chlor-aseptic) can anesthetize her throat and reduce her cough for thirty minutes to two hours while releasing little or no medication into her bloodstream. Tessalon Perles (benzonatate) are helpful if you can find them, and I have never seen them cause problems with bipolar disorder. Make sure your child swallows the capsule and does not suck or chew it.

What can I give my daughter for congestion?

Avoid cold, allergy, and cough medicines that contain the usual deconges-tants, including ephedrine, pseudoephedrine, phenylephrine, and phenyl-propanolamine. These reduce congestion by amping up adrenaline in every cell of your daughter's body. Clearly, this is overkill for children in general and dangerous for your bipolar child. For nasal congestion, you may try saline nasal spray. If this is insufficient, have her try a twelve-hour nasal spray containing oxymetazoline and nothing else. Make sure your daughter does not use it more than necessary so that she does not build up a tolerance. If oxymetazoline nasal spray is not enough, find out if the congestion is relieved by loratadine (Claritin) or diphenhydramine (Benadryl).

What can I give my child for colds and allergies?

Currently my patients are having the best luck with loratadine (Claritin). Diphenhydramine (Benadryl) works better but it may be too sedating (although some children do not notice the sedation at all). Make sure you get these medicines without decongestants, because drug companies like to combine antihistamines with decongestants that increase adrenaline. Recently a mother told me that her daughter had taken Benadryl and become manic and unable to sleep. It turned out that she had inadvertently bought "diphenhydramine with decongestant."

I hear the word "steroids" bantered about on television. Are these bad for my daughter?

That depends on what type of steroids we are talking about. I have seen numerous cases of bipolar depression, mania, and psychosis triggered by anabolic steroids taken for bodybuilding. I have seen more than one case of suicide and murder caused by steroids plus antidepressants. However, your daughter may be able to tolerate the steroids in asthma inhalers or steroid injections like cortisone or prednisone for sports injuries. Let your doctor know that steroid treatments may exacerbate your daughter's bipolar disorder so you can properly weigh the risks.

6.

PSYCHOTHERAPY IS IMPORTANT FOR YOUR CHILD'S BIPOLAR DISORDER

. . . .

Psychotherapy is an essential part of treatment for children with bipolar disorder. Studies have consistently shown that the combination of medications with psychotherapy is better than medications alone. If I were to take on the treatment of your child, I would want to be sure that he or she would be getting psychotherapy as well as medications.

Psychotherapy serves many needs in bipolar treatment. Good therapy can help bipolar children see the reality of their lives more clearly, and receive an appropriate and informed balance of encouragement, objectivity, and focus on the problems at hand. You need to know what kinds of therapy are available and how they work, what types of therapists are available, and how to select them in order to get the best combination for your child.

Which should my son start first: medicine or psychotherapy?

If he cannot start both together, it is best for him to start medication therapy first. That way, your son's mind will be working most efficiently when he starts his psychotherapy, and he will get the most from the experience.

HOW CAN PSYCHOTHERAPY IMPROVE MY CHILD'S BIPOLAR TREATMENT?

. . . . . .

1. You and your child will have more opportunities to be educated about bipolar disorder when you engage in the psychotherapeutic process.
2. Your child will take medications more regularly if he or she is receiving psychotherapy.
3. Psychotherapy reduces the stress that drives your child's bipolar disorder.
4. Discussing communication and social relationships helps your child become more effective and have better interactions with family, friends, teachers, and schoolmates.
5. Sharing anger, jealousy, and resentments with a therapist helps your child contain these negative emotions and reduces the likelihood that they will come out at home or in school. It is better for your child to release anger with a therapist than with you.
6. Psychotherapy gives your bipolar child a chance to model, role-play, and try out attitudes and behaviors on an adult and get their feedback in a safe, supportive environment.
7. Psychotherapists with experience in treating bipolar children will already have behavioral and communication strategies ready to help your child bypass bipolar limitations.

Should we get a separate therapist or ask our psychiatrist to provide my son's therapy, too?

It is completely up to you. All psychiatrists are trained in giving psychotherapy. Your psychiatrist may be interested in doing both or may prefer that you engage a separate therapist for your son. Certainly, your son's psychiatrist already knows about your son's condition and can use the information from psychotherapy to improve medication treatment and vice versa. However, if your child already has a great working relationship with a separate therapist, it may be better to keep the therapist you already have, if he or she is knowledgeable or willing to learn about bipolar disorder and its treatment.

From this point forward, when I say psychiatrist and psychotherapist I will assume that you understand that both may be the same person.

Will my current therapist be able to educate me and my family about my bipolar disorder?

I hope that someday most psychotherapy training programs will teach enough about bipolar disorder to make this possible. Unless your psychotherapist has special experience and training in bipolar disorder, that job will fall to your psychiatrist at this time.

Does my daughter really need to talk with a psychotherapist? Isn't it better for my child to share her secrets with her own mother than with a stranger?

Psychotherapy is much different than a mother talking to her daughter. A strong supportive relationship between you and your daughter is certainly essential for her to thrive. However, psychotherapists study for years to learn and perfect the techniques of behavioral, interpersonal, cognitive, reality, psychodynamic, and other types of therapy that can help your daughter's bipolar disorder. (See pages 151–156 for an explanation of each of the major types of psychotherapy.) Bipolar children also benefit from a safe, therapeutic environment where they can let off steam without the danger of being disrespectful, uncooperative, or irritating to their parents.

How can I tell if my daughter's therapy is working?

If your daughter comes home from her therapy session motivated and more centered in the moment (even if she is irritated or complains about the therapist), then her therapy is working.

CHOOSING A THERAPIST

The most important thing to consider in choosing a therapist is his or her track record. If a therapist has experience with and has consistently helped other children with bipolar disorder, then you probably want him or her to treat your child.

I don't know any therapists. How can I find a good one for my daughter?

Ask your child's psychiatrist, family doctor, and pediatrician if they can refer your daughter to a good therapist whom they have worked with in the past. Ask the mothers of other children with bipolar disorder or similar problems if they like their therapists well enough to recommend them. Go to local meetings of mental health organizations like the National Alliance on Mental Illness (NAMI) and listen to what others say about their children's therapists. See Chapter 12 for more leads.

How do I know if my son's psychiatrist is already giving him psychotherapy? If not, how can I ask him to be my son's therapist?

If your psychiatrist is spending twenty minutes or more with your child, ask if he or she is performing psychotherapy. If so, and you like your son's progress, then you do not need to do anything further. If you think you might like your son's psychiatrist to be his psychotherapist, too, just ask the doctor to discuss this with you.

How do I know if a therapist is qualified to see my son?

Ask them whether they are licensed to practice psychotherapy in your state (some states do not require licensure) and whether they went to an accredited school or training program. Visit the Web site of your state board of medicine, professional psychology, marriage and family counselors, or social workers to find out about licensure and whether programs are accredited. All graduates of a medical psychiatry residency have been to an accredited program. Ask them how long they have been practicing and what type of psychotherapy they have been trained in. If the person is still a student in training, find out the name of their supervisor and, if possible, talk to the supervisor directly.

Can a person just call themselves a therapist without any training in psychotherapy?

Unfortunately, in most states, anyone can put up a sign and call themselves a therapist. Other fancy names like mind/body facilitator, child mental health coach, treatment specialist, etc., may be made up or based on a certificate they received from a questionable program. If you are in any doubt, do not hesitate to ask the prospective therapist specifics about their license, training, and education. See Chapter 12.

What else should I ask them?

Ask them whether they are interested in and informed about bipolar disorder in children, how many bipolar children they have seen and treated, and how many they are treating now. Ask them about their treatment approach for bipolar children. It may be that, in your area, there are no psychologists, social workers, or counselors with significant experience treating bipolar children. In that case, either turn therapy over to your child's psychiatrist or ask potential therapists if they would work closely with your child's psychiatrist to become knowledgeable about the condition and its treatment.

WHICH TYPES OF PSYCHOTHERAPY ARE BEST FOR MY BIPOLAR CHILD?

There are many types of therapy and therapists to choose from. Some therapies are well established and proven to help children, while others are unproven. In particular, psychoeducation, behavioral therapy, and interpersonal therapy have been very helpful to other bipolar children in the past. I also describe some other types of therapy that are less useful for bipolar disorder. Your challenge is to determine which is best for your child.

What is psychoeducation, and how do I get it for my bipolar son?

Educating you and your son about bipolar disorder is such an important part of bipolar psychotherapy that it has its own name. Psychoeducation teaches both of you what bipolar disorder is, what causes it, how to cope with it, how to treat it, and how to make the best use of medications. It provides information on the lifestyle changes that will improve your son's bipolar symptoms, how to keep his bipolar disorder from getting worse, and practical strategies for dealing with problems he is likely to experience. It includes information that will help the rest of your family cope better with your son's condition.

Numerous studies have found that psychoeducation is equal to or better than any other types of psychotherapy for bipolar disorder. At this time, psychiatrists specializing in bipolar disorder are the best ones to provide psychoeducation but I hope that family physicians, pediatricians, professional psychologists, counselors, and social workers will be willing to learn this information to give better help to their bipolar clients.

Would reality therapy be helpful for my bipolar depressed son?

Reality therapy (RT) focuses on current problems and practical ways to overcome them. When your son is able to overcome the challenges in his social relationships, school, and family life, he will feel better about himself while getting more respect and appreciation from others. Reality therapy seeks to make your child more aware of his thoughts and actions so he can change them. RT also helps him recognize fantasies so they will not distract him from his real life. Reality therapists try to steer children away from excuses and a preoccupation with negative emotions.

Why do you recommend that my son's psychotherapist "stay in the present"?

Many good therapists focus on immediate events and interactions happening in the daily lives of their bipolar patients. If your son can find practical strategies to make his life better, he will be happier. If we can help your son develop a better understanding of what the other people in his life are feeling and communicating, then he will be happier and his family will be healthier. This practical approach can help instill hope that your son will be able to solve his life challenges and have a genuinely happy, fulfilling, and successful life, without having to dredge up old memories and past disappointments that can fuel bipolar depression.

What is behavioral therapy? What are its advantages for my bipolar daughter?

Behavioral therapy (BT) uses the understanding of behavior based on scientific research to help your daughter change her moods and outlook. BT begins by teaching her how to relax and counteract daily stress. Then practical behaviors are scheduled for her to reduce her depression and anxiety. This is done without stirring up painful emotions or generating guilt or worries about undesirability and inadequacy. I think that behavioral therapy is great for bipolar children. The behavioral programs I present later in this book are based on behavioral techniques. Unfortunately, there is currently a limited number of therapists who are trained in behavioral therapy, and they may be difficult to find.

What goes on in interpersonal therapy? Would it work for my teenager?

Interpersonal therapy (IPT) was specifically developed for treatment of depression, and it has been shown to be effective in adolescents. IPT examines relationships to improve your bipolar teen's adjustment and coping skills. Increasing the understanding of relationships, social interactions, and communications will dramatically improve the life of your bipolar child. Typically, sessions focus on decreasing family, school, and social conflicts, adapting to change, improving social skills, and dealing with grief. I recommend IPT for children with bipolar disorder, and I use interpersonal techniques in my practice.

What is psychodynamic psychotherapy?

Psychodynamic psychotherapy is an outgrowth of Freudian psychoanalysis that seeks to develop insight. This is done by examining the patient's internal thoughts and emotions in order to clarify their internal conflicts, motivations, explanations, and subconscious defenses. In classical psychodynamic psychotherapy, the therapist is quiet and passive, allowing patients to voice their problems and concerns. Unfortunately, many bipolar children are not good candidates for psychodynamic psychotherapy, and need a higher level of participation from their therapist.

My daughter is so quiet, introverted, and depressed that I don't think any kind of therapy could help her. Could it?

Child psychoanalysis is a process of gradual self-revelation in one or several sessions per week. Psychoanalysis can be Freudian, Jungian, or another type.

I particularly like Jung's sand play techniques for young children, and dream analysis for adolescents, as nonthreatening ways to coax introverted, depressed children out of their shells. You can find out more about these types of therapies in Chapter 12. Unfortunately, child analysts are not always easy to find, and the treatment may be expensive.

What is play therapy?

Play therapy involves the use of toys, blocks, dolls, puppets, drawings, and games to help your child recognize, identify, and verbalize feelings and conflicts. It can be used as a part of psychodynamic or psychoanalytic psychotherapy.

What is cognitive therapy and would you recommend it for my bipolar daughter?

Cognitive therapy identifies bad, unhealthy patterns of thought and teaches children to avoid them. Your daughter would be taught that certain thoughts cause negative feelings and moods, which can then cause depression. Overall, it is a great therapy, but if your bipolar daughter is sensitive, she may interpret comments about her cognition as critical or judgmental. Moreover, if she is just beginning her treatment, it may be nearly impossible for her to keep unwanted, intrusive thoughts out of her mind. It may be better to wait until your daughter is more mature and stable, better able to control her thoughts, and better able to absorb criticism before considering cognitive therapy.

An Internet "expert" said *every* troubled child needs family therapy. Do you agree?

Family therapy sessions consist of brothers, sisters, and parents together in the same room, or of couples having marital problems. When family members can communicate better with the help of a therapist, this approach works well. However, when bipolar children just want to go over and over their long-standing disagreements, indignations, and gripes with their family members during the therapy session, it is not as useful.

My cousin was in group therapy. Would it be good for my bipolar son?

A therapy group is a wonderful place for your son to learn social skills and communication. However, group leaders have told me that bipolar children often refuse to talk, are too sensitive to criticism, try to monopolize the conversation, or are too focused on themselves to do well in groups. Like everything else, the success of group therapy depends on the experience and skill of the group therapist. Group therapists may be trained in inter-personal, psychodynamic, supportive, or other types of therapy that they use in their groups.

What are some other types of therapy used for treating bipolar disorder?

Social rhythm therapy employs some of the scheduling techniques discussed in Chapter 4. Prodrome detection therapy seeks to identify triggers for bipolar episodes and tries to help bipolar individuals prevent them from happening. This does not work so well with children, in my experience, because so many bipolar children have mixed symptoms and do not cycle.

Supportive therapy is the kind offered by therapists in my area. Is this good for treating bipolar disorder?

Supportive therapy includes encouraging, nurturing, and reassuring children that they are capable and will eventually succeed. Unfortunately, bipolar manic children already think they are great and successful, while many bipolar depressed children find the optimism annoying. Honesty and objectivity, rather than optimism, can help bipolar children feel anchored in reality. Also, supportive therapists often ask children to reexperience painful emotions and memories that they are struggling to control.

Could therapy ever be harmful to my bipolar daughter?

Some therapists are trained in techniques that are probably helpful for many children but may not help children with bipolar disorder. For example, some therapists may ask your daughter to relive moments of personal pain, grief, depression, inadequacy, self-doubt, self-criticism, and guilt over and over in order to "process" them. Unfortunately, this causes a lot of stress in bipolar children. Heavy emotions, memories, and thoughts that are stirred up inside your daughter during this kind of therapy may not go away for a long time. If your girl is sensitive, she may be overwhelmed and derailed by these techniques.

Your daughter works hard every day to keep negative emotions, thoughts, and fantasies out of her mind so that she can focus on having a healthy life. If she repeatedly comes home from her therapy session crying, it is time for a change.

I'm a teen interested in hypnosis. I think it would work for me, but is it safe?

I do not recommend hypnosis for children or adolescents with bipolar disorder. Your challenge is to see the world the way it is. Hypnosis is the opposite; it encourages you to create fantasies, and I do not think that is helpful for children with bipolar disorder.

Who's the least expensive for my bipolar son to see, a general psychiatrist, a child psychiatrist, a psychologist, a social worker, a counselor, or my family doctor?

People rack their brains over this one. Would it be more economical to pay a psychiatrist to do medications *and* psychotherapy? Is it better to turn therapy over to a social worker or counselor who charges less than the others?

PSYCHOTHERAPISTS HAVE DIFFERENT TYPES OF EDUCATION AND TRAINING

· · · · · ·

- **Psychiatrists** go to school for at least twelve years. They go to college for four years, then four years of medical school to earn an M.D. degree, and then one additional year of internship in a hospital to earn a license to practice general medicine. Then they complete three or four years of additional training in psychiatry in an accredited hospital. They may elect to spend one to three more years as university fellows to gain higher levels of training and experience. They learn the biology of emotional illness, the nature of medications and how to use them, and how to perform psychotherapy. Because of this extensive training, psychiatrists often charge higher fees than nonmedical therapists in the same community.

- **Child and adolescent psychiatrists** earn an M.D. degree, are licensed to practice medicine, and then receive training in general psychiatry and two years in a training program addressing the theories and methods of child and adolescent psychiatry. Their fees are often higher than those of other psychiatrists.

- **Child psychoanalysts** are clinicians who have sought several years of further training from psychoanalytic programs or institutes. Ask the analyst about the details of his or her training to find out more.

- **Professional psychologists** earn a Ph.D. degree in a four-year graduate program and complete a one-year practical internship. They may be the only sources for behavioral therapy or cognitive therapy in your community. Professional psychologists do not receive extensive training in the causes and physiology of bipolar disorder, and they may not have had experience in recognizing and treating bipolar disorder in children. Professional psychologists' fees are usually less than physicians' and more than those charged by counselors.

- **Mental health nurses** attend either a two- or three-year basic nursing program and choose to earn extra certification in mental health nursing. Many mental health nurses have considerable experience and wisdom about inpatient psychiatric illness.

- **Social workers** receive a master's degree in social work (MSW) and are specially trained in the management of moderate and severe mental illness, particularly within the context of public health. They are usually knowledgeable about federal, state, and local services that can help bipolar children and their families. They are usually trained in family therapy and supportive therapy types. Licensed clinical social workers

Continued

(LCSW) have special training in psychotherapy and mental illness. Some social workers provide their services at low or deferred cost.

- **Marriage and family therapists or counselors** usually complete a two-year master's degree (M.A.). They are often trained in family therapy and supportive therapy styles. Counselors usually receive little or no training in recognizing or treating bipolar disorder, and no training in bipolar biology or physiology. A few have worked closely with bipolar children and have experience in their treatment. Family counselors' fees are usually lower than the fees charged by psychiatrists and professional psychologists.

The solution is that whatever keeps your son the healthiest is the least expensive treatment. There are experienced and effective professionals available at all levels, in private practice, HMOs, and community clinics. However, if your son is poorly treated, he may need extra appointments, second opinions, special tutors, or hospitalization, and these costs mount up. Severe illness can deplete your savings, disturb the cohesion of your family, detract from your work performance, or even require a parent to stay home to look after your son.

If you can find professionals who are experienced enough to recognize common bipolar problems and have solutions ready for them, your child will spend less time in bed and more time living a normal life. The way to save money is to get the best treatment for your child.

What kind of therapist can teach my daughter relaxation and stress-reduction techniques?

Behavioral therapists usually teach relaxation and stress-reduction techniques, although any other therapist can learn these and teach them to your daughter. Chapter 4 contains techniques you can learn and teach your daughter that will help both of you relax and reduce your stress.

Q Why do you focus on therapists' education? I heard that the degree isn't that important.

Professional credentials give you a good idea of the level and type of specialized training and experience a therapist has had in helping bipolar children. I have heard therapists say that "after the first year of experience, your education doesn't matter," but I do not find this to be the case. In fact, I always have to add to my education by reading journals and listening to lectures in an attempt to keep current on the latest treatment methods for bipolar children.

Q Can psychologists prescribe drugs? Who can legally prescribe medications for my child?

A few states have given psychologists limited prescribing privileges, but in most states only medical doctors can prescribe medicines.

HOW TO HELP YOUR CHILD WITH BEHAVIORAL PROGRAMS AT HOME

You or a family member can help your bipolar child at home and complement his or her psychotherapy. I have prepared behavioral programs specifically for bipolar children to help decrease depression, better appreciate life, and do more things that are positive every day. These behavioral programs do not take the place of one-to-one contact with a real behavioral therapist, but they may fill the gap if your child's therapist does not do behavioral work or is away on vacation, or if no therapist is available in your area. If your son has a therapist, bring the program work sheets to his session. The work sheets may provide interesting material to discuss, and the therapist may wish to work them into your son's psychotherapy treatment.

The Pleasant Events Program Can Reduce
Your Bipolar Child's Depression

In bipolar depression, there is a tendency to isolate oneself and avoid doing activities that are pleasant and enjoyable. By contrast, research has shown that doing happy, positive activities can improve a depressed child's outlook on life. The Pleasant Events Program (PEP) is designed to help your bipolar depressed child do more happy activities. This helps her get out and about, and it encourages her to take an active role in making her life better. It can reduce bipolar depression while it discourages isolation, alienation, and feelings that everything is hopeless and nothing is worthwhile. If your child can be more thankful for the wonderful things in his or her life and act more constructively, then your child's attitude and mood will get better and life will be happier and more successful.

How can my son and I put the Pleasant Events Program into action?

Carefully remove the PEP work sheet from this book and make copies. Then sit down and go through the PEP work sheet with your son. Make a check mark next to any activities he likes to do or thinks that he might like to do. See if you and he can think of other enjoyable things and add them to the list. Then, every Sunday night, look at the list and make plans to do some of the activities in the coming week. Every time your son completes an activity on the list, the date should be filled in on the work sheet.

How do I know if PEP is working for my son's depression?

Initially scheduling and participating in pleasant activities may be difficult for your child because of his depression. As he participates in this program, you should see your son wanting to do more pleasant things, first with encouragement and then more spontaneously. If you check the work sheet and find that it is filled out with many activities and many dates, the program is working. If not, you should reassure him that, although his depression makes it difficult to participate in pleasant activities, forcing himself to experience happy events should help him feel better.

The Pleasant Events Program

Check all the activities you like to do or think you would like to do. Add your own favorites. Then plan when you will do these activities and fill in the dates when you do them.

DATES YOU DID THEM:

Going to the mall

Going to a concert

Visiting a museum

Going bowling

Going to a movie

Going to the park

Going to the zoo

Going to a sporting event

Renting a movie

Going out with friends

Calling a distant relative

Going camping

Visiting someone out of town

Eating at a restaurant

Going hiking

Going over to a friend's home

Going to church or temple

Going to the library

Going on a drive

Flying a kite

Going to a party

Visiting a parent at work

Spending the night with a friend

Making a present for someone

Taking photographs

Doing your own artwork

Playing a musical instrument

Going to a play

Cooking a meal

Eating a meal with friends

_____

_____

_____

_____

_____

Color My World Programs One and Two

Color My World Program One helps your child *notice* the profound yet simple beauty all around, which he might otherwise have missed because of bipolar depressed or manic symptoms. It provides him with believable and graphic proof that good things are happening, and it blocks the bipolar tendency to turn inward and overfocus on himself. By getting him to look outside himself, Color My World Program One helps him engage with the real world instead of internal fantasies.

Color My World Program Two helps your child *take actions* that improve his world. It gives your child proof that he can cause good things to happen and stops your child from doubting his ability to make himself happy. By helping your child see how his actions can affect the way he feels, Color My World Program Two encourages your child to play an active role in his life and in his health.

To begin, carefully remove the Color My World Program One and Two work sheets from this book and make copies. Programs One and Two alternate each week. Always use a new copy of the work sheets every week. Encourage your child to come up with new items he likes to see and do, and feel free to change items on the list as his needs and interests change.

How do my daughter and I put the Color My World Program One into action?

On the first week, sit down with your child and examine the Color My World Program One work sheet together. Review every item on the work sheet and, if appropriate, discuss each one briefly. Ask your daughter which items she enjoys the most. Starting with the current day, see which of the items on the list she has noticed lately and check them off on the work sheet. Then, sit down quietly with your daughter after dinner or before she goes to bed each evening and go through the list with her, checking every item she noticed that day. Some children will want to discuss these events with you at this time. At the end of the week, you may comment on how many items your child noticed that week. Often, older children will complete the work sheet on their own and, if they do not wish to converse about the results, it is not necessary to comment on them.

Color My World Program One

This week, check the things you have *noticed* that make your life more enjoyable.
Feel free to add other things you have noticed and enjoyed.

MON TUE WED THU FRI SAT SUN

Check each day:

you noticed feeling good
you had something to look forward to
someone said something nice to you
you found out good news
you found something amusing
you saw something pretty
you heard a good joke
someone showed you they love you
someone helped you
you enjoyed being by yourself
something made you feel happy
you received a gift
you enjoyed being with others
it was nice outdoors
someone showed they were your friend
you watched the sun rise or set
you recalled a pleasant memory
you saw a nice flower or plant
you looked at the clouds
you enjoyed listening to music
you looked at the stars or moon
you were appreciated by others
you were around happy people
you felt love for someone
you noticed someone for the first time
you saw a happy face
you enjoyed exercising
you met someone new
you felt your strength
you had a pleasant spiritual experience
you noticed you were relaxed
you felt thankful for all the good things

_____
_____
_____
_____

MON TUE WED THU FRI SAT SUN

What should my son and I do with the Color My World Program Two?

On the second week, sit down with your son and examine the Color My World Program Two work sheet together. As with Program One, review each item on the work sheet and discuss each one briefly. Beginning with the current day, see which items on the list your son has already done and check them off on the work sheet. Then go through the list quietly with your child each evening after dinner or before he goes to bed, checking each thing on the list that he did that day. Your son may want to discuss the list with you at this time. At the end of the week, you may comment on whether there are many or few actions that he has taken that week. If your son is older, he may complete the work sheet on his own and he may not want to discuss the results.

How do my son and I continue to use the Color My World Programs?

Keep alternating Color My World Programs One and Two weekly to keep the program interesting and to emphasize that we both experience beauty and do things that enhance the beauty of our lives. Save the old work sheets in a folder so you and your son can examine them monthly and keep track of his improvement.

THE STAGES OF THE BIPOLAR RECOVERY PROGRAM

Attitude is important, and I am often asked what kind of attitude children with bipolar disorder need to beat their condition. I have divided the recovery process into four steps for your child to complete, along with affirmations that will help him progress to full health and maintain it. Read or show these steps to your young child every Sunday and have him say the affirmations with you at that time. Focus on each step one at a time. Older children should copy down each step and affirmation and put the paper in

Color My World Program Two

This week, check the things you have *done* that make your life more enjoyable. Feel free to add other things you have done and enjoyed.

	Mon	Tue	Wed	Thu	Fri	Sat	Sun
Check each day you:							
did something healthy	—	—	—	—	—	—	—
played some pleasant music	—	—	—	—	—	—	—
went to a place you like	—	—	—	—	—	—	—
told someone you love them	—	—	—	—	—	—	—
did something pleasant for yourself	—	—	—	—	—	—	—
played with your pet	—	—	—	—	—	—	—
drank a beverage that you like	—	—	—	—	—	—	—
made something beautiful	—	—	—	—	—	—	—
ate a favorite meal	—	—	—	—	—	—	—
had an interesting new thought	—	—	—	—	—	—	—
put on clothes you like	—	—	—	—	—	—	—
kissed someone	—	—	—	—	—	—	—
said something amusing	—	—	—	—	—	—	—
read something pleasant	—	—	—	—	—	—	—
showed someone that you care	—	—	—	—	—	—	—
had a friendly conversation	—	—	—	—	—	—	—
wrote for pleasure	—	—	—	—	—	—	—
were a good listener	—	—	—	—	—	—	—
told a good joke	—	—	—	—	—	—	—
took a pleasant walk	—	—	—	—	—	—	—
ate a tasty snack	—	—	—	—	—	—	—
took a pleasant nap	—	—	—	—	—	—	—
read a book for fun	—	—	—	—	—	—	—
talked to friends	—	—	—	—	—	—	—
made someone happy	—	—	—	—	—	—	—
worked on a puzzle	—	—	—	—	—	—	—
had a meaningful conversation	—	—	—	—	—	—	—
helped someone else	—	—	—	—	—	—	—
touched someone you care for	—	—	—	—	—	—	—
learned something new	—	—	—	—	—	—	—
created something new	—	—	—	—	—	—	—
solved a difficult problem	—	—	—	—	—	—	—
_____	—	—	—	—	—	—	—
_____	—	—	—	—	—	—	—
_____	—	—	—	—	—	—	—
_____	—	—	—	—	—	—	—

	Mon	Tue	Wed	Thu	Fri	Sat	Sun

a prominent place where they can see the step and say the affirmation every day. As you are convinced that your child has mastered the current step, help him progress to the next.

THE FOUR STEPS OF
BIPOLAR RECOVERY IN CHILDREN

**First Step: Accepting that you must take your
medication even if you do not want to.**
Affirmation: "Even though I do not understand
it now, this is something I must do."

**Second Step: Accepting that you must do what
your parents and other authorities tell you.**
Affirmation: "I must follow the rules, even if I do not agree with them."

**Third Step: Accepting that what you think and
feel does not control what you do.**
Affirmation: "Whether I think I am perfect or a failure
I must still do what is expected of me."

Fourth Step: (For older children): **Accepting that you play
an important role in your family, your school, and your society.**
Affirmation: "I take responsibility for the choices I make
and the consequences of what I do."

7.

PRACTICAL STRATEGIES
FOR PARENTING YOUR
BIPOLAR CHILD

. . . .

Having a bipolar child is a challenge for the entire family. Parents of bipolar children must attend to their needs as well as those of their other family members and themselves. Problems with eating and other habits, childhood struggles with authority, and emerging issues of maturing sexuality create a big demand on parenting skills. At the same time, parents must take good care of their own health, keep their marriage solid, and have enough time and space to live their own lives.

HEALING THE FAMILY

The first step in helping your family heal is enabling everybody to understand what's going on with your bipolar child. Find material for your spouse and other children to read (such as this book) and give family members the Internet addresses for bipolar Web sites that offer family support (see Chapter 12). Subscribe to bipolar magazines and newsletters for you and your family to read. Have a family conference in which you clarify that if family members have questions about bipolar disorder, you and your child's doctor can help find the answers.

How old should my son be before I can explain bipolar disorder to him?

I think many children can begin to understand their condition by age seven and begin to take an active role in their treatment by age ten. Do not try to pile on the information; just let them know that they have a health condition that needs treatment so they can be happy and healthy. Offer to answer their questions and show them this book if they are old enough, but do not be surprised if they do not want to know very much at this time.

Shouldn't we try to hide from the family the fact that something is wrong with our daughter?

If you try to keep everything hushed up, you send the message that your daughter's condition is so horrible that it cannot be named or discussed. When you and your family members can talk about the condition in a practical and matter-of-fact manner, it shows her that no one is scared or embarrassed by her bipolar condition.

What about telling others outside the family?

I generally advise families to treat bipolar disorder as family business, not to be discussed outside the home. However, bipolar disorder is common enough that many children talk about it together on their own.

How do I explain to my other children about their sister's bipolar disorder?

You can tell them that their sister has an illness that starts in childhood and requires treatment, patience, and support from her family members. Stress that, under good circumstances, her life will be just like everyone else's. Mention that this condition makes it necessary for you to give her extra help and attention periodically, but that you love everyone equally.

How can I get the rest of my family to accept that my son is ill? Frankly, I need their support.

One of the best ways to gain acceptance and support for your bipolar son's condition is to involve the family in helping each other. Older brothers and sisters can be assigned specific tasks, like coaching your son in his homework, helping him practice sports, or getting him ready for school. Assign your bipolar son the job of helping his younger brother(s) and sister(s) do their homework, get ready for bed, or do their exercises. In this way, everyone is involved and everyone gets to know and understand their family members better. In the process, the family will become aware of your son's special needs and vulnerabilities.

Our bipolar son complains that it is not fair that his older sister is getting awards and having parties for her graduation. How do we explain this to him?

Explain to your son that everyone is different and everyone has rewards and successes according to their own age, interests, and talents. Stress that he has had and will have rewards and successes of his own to celebrate.

Why does my son have to fight with his brothers and sisters?

Irritability is one of the most consistent features of bipolar disorder at all ages, during both depression and mania. Anger episodes and fights can materialize and escalate in the wink of an eye. Bring this problem to the attention of your son's doctor and therapist and ask what they can do to reduce his anger. Check with other parents of bipolar children on Internet support groups to see which strategies they have developed to reduce fighting.

Q I spend all my time helping my bipolar son. I am exhausted with no life of my own. Help!

Make sure you have the help of your child's psychiatrist, therapist, and school, as well as your own family members and friends. Decide what is reasonable for you to do personally and how much you can turn over to professionals and other family members. Remember, you must look after your own health if you are to help your son.

Grief and Loss

Cause and effect may be unclear to bipolar children, and they often get the idea that events around them happen randomly and without warning. It is terrifying when they realize that they live in a world where anyone can suddenly be sucked out of life without cause or warning.

Q How can I help my young bipolar child deal with the concepts of death and separation?

These concepts are often too complex for younger children. It is better to focus on how we will get on with our lives and be happy even though our loved ones will no longer be with us. I say, "After we lose someone, it's good to know that we can go back to our regular life again and do all the happy things we used to do."

My son broke up with his girlfriend and he is not coping well. What can we do?

Vulnerability to stress and a resistance to change can make the breakup with a friend a devastating experience for bipolar children. To a bipolar child, the loss of a loved one can leave an empty hole that feels like it can never be filled. Your best bet is to help your son become involved in social activities with other people again. Take him out to movies and athletic games with the family, go to church, drive him to the park, invite his friends over, and help fill up that empty spot.

FAITH AND THE FAMILY

Faith and spiritual belief are important parts of our lives. You should draw strength from your spiritual practices and use them to help your bipolar child and to unite the rest of your family.

Our minister wants to help our family, but what can he do?

Your minister can help by ministering to your faith; helping the family become involved in church, family, and community functions; and involving your children in youth groups and choir.

Our daughter has become really religious. It's odd because we're not a very religious family.

Bipolar disorder can cause children to become extremely religious. Religion can give your daughter inner strength, spiritual direction, and fulfillment, as well as a connection with her family roots and values. However, if the bipolar influence is too strong, her religious belief can become obsessional or delusional. The general rule is that if your child is keeping pace with the rules and practices of your religion and community, then things are okay.

Q Every evening we meditate as a family, but our bipolar son is too distracted. Suggestions?

Your son may have a difficult time controlling his thoughts, keeping focused, and keeping stray thoughts out of his conscious mind. If your son cannot meditate the way the rest of your family members do, give him the option of reading, or thinking about spiritual principles. Then work with your son's doctor until your son's thought control is stronger and he can share the same spiritual experience that you do.

EATING PROBLEMS

Eating problems are an integral part of bipolar disorder. Bipolar manic children may eat less, bipolar depressed children may eat more, and as it was for Goldilocks, it is a challenge to get their meals "just right."

Q Our daughter is so picky about food that she's getting painfully thin. What can we do about this?

Picky eating is hard to treat, and can result in unhealthy weight loss. Once your daughter feels nausea or gags while eating a food, these sensations tend to recur and she will begin avoiding that food. See if your daughter's psychotherapist can help her lower the stress around meals. Meanwhile, try to make sure she gets enough protein by including chicken, beef, dairy foods, eggs, fish, tofu, or turkey in her diet.

Q My son takes hours to pick at his food, but he wants the family to stay at the table until he's decided he's through. We try to comply because we want him to eat more, but it is interfering with our lives. Suggestions?

By using his slow, inadequate eating to become the center of attention and control the family, your son is rewarded for his poor food intake. This will not help him eat more normally. Instead, have your other family members ignore your bipolar son's slowness and leave the table as soon as they finish their own food so he will not have an audience. If your son does not finish his food in a reasonable time, clear the table. When he gets hungry you can negotiate what food he will receive and when.

Q I try to push my son to eat more, but he just gives up after a few bites. Help!

If pushing does not work, change tactics. Notice how much your son eats tonight, and tomorrow serve him only the same amount he ate before. If he asks for more, tell him you are pleased, but never give him more than you are sure he will eat right away. Try this for a while and see if his eating habits improve.

Q My five-year-old can never make up his mind. We take him out to dinner and I go through the whole menu but I can't get him to tell me what he wants. When he finally picks something and the food arrives, he says he doesn't like it and he won't eat it. What do you suggest?

Choosing restaurant food may be too big a task at this age. Just order something on the menu you think he will like. If he does not eat it, give him some food he likes when you get home. To avoid wasting his restaurant meal, you can have it wrapped up and take it home for the doggie (or for you).

HELP FOR HABITS AND MOVEMENTS

Bipolar children of all ages are especially vulnerable to developing bad habits and compulsive behaviors.

Q Do you have any suggestions to help stop my daughter's fingernail-biting habit?

Nail biting can cause infections and malformations of the nail. However, it only increases in response to stress and attention, so reminding or nagging just makes it worse. Instead, try mixing a solution of quinine in water, the same sort of solution that pet stores sell to stop dogs from chewing or biting themselves. Try wiping this on your daughter's fingers. It is so bitter that when she puts a fingertip in her mouth, she will be reminded not to bite her nails. Over time, this can help her learn to curb her biting habit. If your daughter is older, try to have her bite a knuckle when she feels the urge to chew her fingernails, or confine her biting to just one nail.

Q Our son spends his homework time playing computer games. What do you recommend?

Computer games can become a habit but, contrary to popular opinion, they are not essential to human life. Instead of arguing, just uninstall games that are on the computer, collect game consoles, and take away electronic devices during study time.

Q I am constantly counting things or tapping out a rhythm in my head. What's this about?

Counting and tapping are surprisingly common in bipolar disorder. Although you may be concerned, it usually causes no harm. If you want to make it go away, I suggest you try the behavioral program described on page 176.

Q Our son sniffs and coughs continually. What is this?

These may be tics, which are short or incomplete behaviors that occur repeatedly with no purpose. Tics occur unconsciously and increase with stress, so it does not help to tell your son not to perform them. Mostly, tics should be ignored if they do not hurt your child.

Q These tics are making me self-conscious at school. What can I do to stop them?

Keep away from stimulants like caffeine (found in sodas, coffee, etc.), which increase tics. Make sure you are getting enough sleep. Do relaxation exercises or meditation to reduce your stress during the day and try our behavioral program to reduce unwanted behaviors. If the problem does not go away, discuss it with your doctor. Some medications (such as clonidine) can reduce tics.

A BEHAVIORAL PROGRAM TO EXTINGUISH BOUNCING LEGS, TICS, COUNTING, AND SIMILAR HABITS

1. Start by realizing that your subconscious mind controls most of your behavior, but it does not know what you want it to do and it is not helping you extinguish your unwanted habits.
2. The first step in reprogramming your behavior is to inform your subconscious mind that you want it to help curb this undesired habit. When you notice an unwanted behavior, give yourself an upbeat message. Say or whisper something positive like "I want my leg to remain quiet," "I no longer bite my nails," or "I am done with clearing my throat."
3. If this is not enough and your subconscious mind is still not paying attention, you can provide a wake-up call. Put a loose rubber band around your wrist and snap it lightly while saying your message to the subconscious mind. Just snap hard enough that you can clearly feel it; this is not a punishment by rubber band. If you do not like the rubber band, try biting a knuckle lightly or squeezing your thumbnail lightly.
4. Be consistent, be matter-of-fact, but do not be critical of yourself. I have helped people erase habits of twenty years with this method, so just take it easy, and send your message.

CHILDHOOD STRUGGLES WITH AUTHORITY

Defiance, resentment, and problems with authority are expressions of anger. Anger can be adjusted closer to normal levels with medications and psychotherapy, so contact your psychiatrist and therapist, and ask them to help with your child's anger through medication adjustment and an anger-management program.

Q My son gets in trouble because he says nobody
has the right to tell him what to do.
What now?

Of course you have the right to tell your son what to do, and so do any other adults in authority. Try to make it clear to your son that he is a child and will be under the control of adults until he is mature. Remember that it is not a negotiation; you already have the power.

Q My son says we have no right to go in his
room and check his stuff. What do we
tell him?

This situation frequently becomes the turning point in the treatment of older bipolar children. Bipolar children often exercise poor judgment and, as the parent, you must monitor what they are doing. If your child is hiding unfinished assignments, notes from the teacher or principal, or evidence of forbidden activities like drinking or other drug use, this is an opportunity for you to stop a problem before it goes too far. If you check his room and do not find anything objectionable, then you have done your job as a parent and you can breathe a sigh of relief.

Q Why does my daughter try to control what
everyone in our family does? She even
decides what we wear.

Bipolar disorder can turn children into little tyrants. In addition to your family, teachers and other adults will resent your daughter if she tries to exert control over them, and she will lose friends who do not want to be bossed around. The best thing for family members to do is to ignore your daughter's bossy behavior. Do not reply and do not change what you are doing. Do not resist, fight, or engage your daughter; just do not do what she says.

Why does the school tell me my child is disruptive in class? He doesn't seem disruptive to me.

You need to go to the school and sit in on your son's classes to find out what is going on. Children sometimes talk out of turn, talk in class, move around, or do disruptive things that you may not see at home. Even if your child shapes up temporarily while you are observing, you will still have made a significant statement to your child and the teacher that you are concerned with and involved in your child's actions.

What does the school mean when they say my daughter has "behavioral problems"?

The term "behavioral problems" is usually a euphemism applied to children who speak inappropriately, disdain authority, and disrupt classes or other school activities. You can see how uncomfortable this is for teachers, who have a big investment in their ability to keep their classes under control. It does not matter what excuses your daughter makes for her behavior; it shows disrespect and teachers will resent it. Bring your doctor and therapist in on this problem and check Internet support groups to see what strategies other parents have found for their children's behavioral problems.

What can we do with our bipolar daughter on our family outings? She ruins everything.

Family outings can be a challenge for children with bipolar disorder because of the stress resulting from the extra stimulation and the change of routine. Until she is more resistant to stress, it may be necessary for your daughter to stay at home or for the family to pick another type of activity that she cannot ruin.

TANTRUMS

Of all the emotions that may get out of control in your child's bipolar disorder, anger is the most destructive to relationships, property, and your child's well-being. If your child seldom throws a tantrum, you can simply throw your arms around her and tell her you love her, and the tantrum will often cease. However, if your child throws frequent tantrums, there is the danger that rageful acts will become a habitual response to frustration. In this case, you need to help your child learn to recover from tantrums on her own.

My bipolar daughter has tantrums and I can't stand it anymore. What can I do?

If this is a mild outbreak, just ignore her. Remember that your daughter is throwing this tantrum in order to get a reaction from *you*. (Otherwise, she would be throwing it in front of somebody else or when she is alone in her room.) If you do not react, the tantrum is no longer working to get a reaction from you and it will eventually begin to fade.

Be serious about not reacting. When your daughter has a tantrum, do not talk to her, answer her questions, or even look in her direction until she begins acting properly. Then go back to your usual interaction as a parent.

What if ignoring my son just makes him madder?

At first, ignoring your son during a tantrum *may* provoke a stronger reaction. Your son may accuse, cry, placate, plead, scream, yell, jump up and down, or lie down and kick his arms and legs in the air. He will do everything imaginable to get you to continue fighting with him, but do not give in to these ploys. Keep pretending he is not even in the room. Only begin interacting with him when he has completely calmed down. You did not cause the tantrum and you do not have to fix it. Just stop being part of it and wait until it blows over.

What if my daughter's tantrum becomes too severe? I'm afraid she'll break something.

If your daughter's tantrum is too serious to be ignored, then she needs more help. Insist that she go to a quiet place and remain there until she is back in control. Learn the "One, Two, Three" rule. You give two warnings and if your daughter acts out again, out she goes. Make sure you impose the time-outs immediately, while she still remembers why they are being given. When she is by herself, separated from you, the tantrum will fade. This separation will also give you a chance to calm down.

After the tantrum is over, insist that your daughter pay for any of your property she has broken or damaged, either in money or in extra chores.

What keeps my son's tantrums going?

Your interaction keeps them going. He wants a big reaction from you. When you participate in an argument, you are further fueling the tantrums. When you try to console or reason with your son, you are fueling the tantrums. Whether you exhibit emotions of anger and yell, or you exhibit emotions of sadness and cry, you are throwing fuel on the fire. Your son is desperately trying to connect with you and communicate with you, but he can't do it until he calms down.

What in the world does my son want to communicate by throwing a tantrum?

Your son wants to share this huge, intolerable emotion of rage with you in the hope that you will be able to make it go away. Sometimes the only emotion that a bipolar child has is rage, and when he shares his feelings with you, that is what you get. Even though you seem omnipotent to your son, you cannot get into his mind and stop the rage. Until he is mature enough to control his own anger, you just have to sit back and wait.

Don't be fooled into thinking that you are the source of the problem or even that the subject of your disagreement is the source of the problem. In a bipolar tantrum, your son's internal supply of anger becomes so strong that he cannot stand it. All he can do is show you his rage.

What if my daughter throws a tantrum in a public place?

If she cannot get her rage under control after two warnings, then your daughter will have to leave the scene. If she is older, consider whether it is safe for her to go wait in the car briefly. Sometimes you will have to drive her home and have her go to her room. The next time a public outing is planned, she may have to stay home.

My son's tantrums are much worse than the ones you have described. Is there anything else we can do?

In addition to the tantrum-reducing behaviors discussed above, ask his therapist to start anger-management therapy. Also, talk to your doctor about whether a time-out medication is necessary. Many children can take a short nap and awaken calm and reasonable again, to everyone's relief.

Things looked good for months, but then my child had another tantrum. What's the use?

Be patient. Tantrums do not suddenly go away. Improvement is measured by how quickly your child recovers each time and how far apart the tantrums are. Do not lose hope or try to change the treatment because of one incident.

Correcting Bipolar Children's Behavior
The most important role in correcting bipolar children's behavior is to get them to pause, notice the problems they are causing, and make a mental note not to repeat them in the future. If your child is upset, wait a few

moments until she is calm, or give her a brief time-out. Then it is time to make the correction. We call it the correction because you tell your child the correct thing to do.

How do you recommend that we correct our bipolar son?

Corrections must be made without criticizing, berating, becoming angry, or making your son feel guilty. Wait until you are calm, keep your manner matter-of-fact, and avoid becoming adversarial. Then, relax and 1) tell him *exactly* what you want him to do, 2) offer your help if the task proves too difficult, and 3) tell him what the consequences will be if he does not perform the task you request. This is the correction, and it is what helps your child learn.

For example, do not tell your son, "Billy, why can't you be responsible? You're acting like a two-year-old. When will you ever grow up? You made your little sister cry." This can make your child more angry, or guilty, or puzzled, but it does not tell him what you want him to do. Instead, relax and say, "Billy, I want you to clean up the mess and replace the broken cup by this time tomorrow. If you need help, let me know, because I don't want you to have further consequences."

Or calmly say, "Billy, I want you to stop hitting your sister. If you need help with her, bring the problem to me. If I have to mention it again tonight, you will not watch television."

Or try saying matter-of-factly, "Billy, your father and I want you to get better grades and so we want you to do your homework. If you need more help with homework, tell me. I am going to check your homework every morning, and any day that it is not done you will have to come home straight after school."

Do you see how this works? You get your message across without accusations, anger, criticism, personal comments, or value judgments, and you make it crystal clear what he is to do and what will happen if he does not do it.

My daughter always says that it wasn't her fault. What then?

It does not matter whether your daughter blames her mistake on her brother, the school, the teacher, or you. If she has been part of a mistake, then she needs to take part in the correction. It is not up for discussion.

SEXUALITY AND BIPOLAR DISORDER IN CHILDREN

Sex drive often increases during bipolar disorder, especially during mania. When this occurs suddenly and out of social context, it can take children and parents by surprise.

Is my daughter sexually vulnerable because of her bipolar disorder?

In addition to increasing her sex drive, bipolar disorder can also impair your daughter's thought process so that she has difficulty telling when situations are risky or male friends are unreliable. Bipolar impulsivity and poor judgment can then lead to unsafe decisions. If you add alcohol or marijuana, this creates an even more dangerous situation.

My son's behavior has become much more sexual in the last two weeks. Is it bipolar disorder?

Bipolar disorder can make your son's sexual drive go up and down suddenly and dramatically. This can be distracting, confusing, or dangerous, depending on the situation. If your son's sexual behavior interferes with his schoolwork or home life, you need to ask your psychiatrist and therapist to help stabilize his sexual drive.

Q My teenaged son confided in me that he is a sex addict. It's all he thinks about all day long.

Having lots of sexual thoughts and urges is not unusual for adolescents, especially boys. However, if these sexual thoughts are interfering with his life and he cannot bring them under control on his own, ask him to mention the problem to his doctor and therapist.

Q Once a year my daughter starts wearing perfume, makeup, and low tops. Then a week later, she has a manic episode. What is this?

Bipolar disorder may begin to drive up your daughter's sexual drive before her manic cycle starts. Now that you know what is going on, you may be able to use these changes as an advanced warning that her manic cycle is about to start. When you see your daughter begin to act this way, make an appointment with her psychiatrist and see if a temporary medication change can block the occurrence of her mania.

Q I found pornography in my son's computer. What should I do?

In my opinion, children should not have access to pornography. However, if it is on the Internet, they will find it, and it may be especially distracting to children with bipolar disorder. I suggest that you approach the problem calmly and with common sense. Sit down with your son and tell him that viewing pornography is not appropriate. Tell him that you would prefer that he did something more productive with his time. Put his computer in a more public area, show interest in the Web sites he visits, and help him use the Internet the way it should be used, for study and schoolwork.

PARENTS HAVE THEIR OWN CHALLENGES

First and foremost, be a loving parent. Your family needs your love, so avoid sidetracking yourself by taking on the work of the doctor, therapist, teacher, or social worker. Ally yourself with these people and ensure that they do the work that is their responsibility, so you can be the best parent possible. Your child may not remember what happened this day or that, but your child will always remember that you were a loving and caring parent.

Are you sure I haven't given my child bipolar disorder by bad parenting?

You can be sure of it. If you have any parenting regrets, erase them by being a great parent right now.

My spouse and I love our bipolar child deeply, but she doesn't seem to love us. Suggestions?

It is sometimes hard for bipolar children to feel love when they are angry, depressed, or focused inward on themselves. Do not forget that your child is a child. She will remember how you love her now and, when she is mature, healthy, and under control, you will be there to see her outpouring of love for you and the rest of her family.

I feel so guilty because sometimes I don't think I like my child. Is this normal?

Face it, you can love your children and spouse, but you cannot like them all the time. Bipolar children are often irritating, exasperating, and just plain impossible. I give you permission to dislike your child sometimes. Just focus on your love for your child instead.

My husband and I love each other, but we
fight. Should I try to keep this from
the kids?

You have to be yourself if you want your family to be healthy. If you try to
act unnaturally, it just confuses your children and makes them question their
own perceptions. If you are cranky or have relationship problems, get these
attended to for the sake of your own health and that of your marriage.

My child's bipolar disorder is ruining my
relationship with my wife. What do
you suggest?

The two of you need to look for support outside your family in mutual
friends, your neighborhood, community activities, and your religion or spiritual practices. Do not let yourselves become isolated from the rest of the
adult world. Pick a night every week to do something fun together without the kids. Bring some romance back into your lives. If one or both of
you have become run-down or depressed, seek professional help and do what
is necessary to be healthy again.

Can you suggest some ways that my wife and
I can stop fighting over our child?

You have to sit down somewhere quiet and make some compromises. Negotiate so that each of you gets something that you want, and let the other
issues go. I have been helping parents do this kind of negotiating successfully for years, so I know it can be done.

If you cannot resolve your differences by yourselves, get help. Nobody
wants to go into couples counseling, but many are glad that they did.

Q My wife is doing all the wrong things with our bipolar son. What can I do?

You can tell your spouse your opinion, you can invite her to consult the doctor and therapist, and you can offer to form a consensus. After that, you have to keep your nose out. All parents have a right to raise their child the way they wish, within the constraints of the law. Besides, it is good for children to see their parents behaving honestly as different people, doing different things. If your son learns to get along with a difficult parent, it is wonderful training for dealing with all the other difficult people he will meet in the course of his life.

Q My wife says our son is sick, but I think he's just lazy and conning her. What do you think?

Usually, there is a little bit of both going on. The real issue is how you can get your son back on track, regardless of what's wrong. Just telling your son to act the way you want is not going to work. If motivation or punishment does not work, then change strategies. Look for practical solutions in your own mind or in this book and put them into action. You have no right to complain unless you are doing something to make the situation better.

Q Do you think I might have bipolar disorder like my child? I'm starting to wonder.

It is a simple thing to check it out. Often parents have a minor version of their children's problems that comes out strongest under stress.

Q I'm a bipolar parent. How can I be healthier so I can parent my son better?

Take the time and energy to look after your own health. You cannot be of any use to your son if you are sick, but if you maintain your health you can be an example to him and to the rest of your family. Reduce stress and get exercise, good nutrition, and recreational time for yourself. If you have medical or emotional problems, begin the work to make yourself healthier. If you have spiritual beliefs, then practice them. If you have friends or contacts in the community, interact with them. Show your son that you can always be happy in the face of adversity and he will strive to follow your example for the rest of his life. If you wish, consult my book on adult bipolar disorder, *The Bipolar Handbook* (Chapter 12).

8.

UNDERSTAND HOW
YOUR BIPOLAR
CHILD THINKS

. . . .

As parents, you know that bipolar disorder causes changes in the brain that affect the way your child thinks. Bipolar thinking problems make it hard for your child to learn from his past experiences, and color his understanding of his own world and the people in it. Understanding how your bipolar son thinks will lead to better communication between you and him and a clearer understanding of why he acts the way he does.

PROBLEMS WITH CAUSE, EFFECT, AND STEPWISE THINKING

The dysfunction of bipolar brain cells makes it hard for bipolar children to perform linear, stepwise information processing and, consequently, they have difficulty understanding the linear phenomena of cause and effect.

Why does my bipolar son give up whenever he runs into a setback?

Bipolar children have difficulty with cause, effect, and linear, stepwise thinking. If your son runs into a problem, he may get stuck and be unable to figure out what to do next because he cannot visualize the next step. Inside your son's mind, it seems like, "If what I want is not happening now, it is never going to happen." Eventually he gets into the habit of giving up.

Why isn't my daughter more patient?

All children can be impatient, but in bipolar children a poor sense of the passage of time can make a few minutes feel like an eternity. A seven-year-old explained it to me like this, "Doctor, can't you see? **I CAN'T WAIT!**"

Because your daughter cannot visualize the next step in her activities, it is very difficult for her to wait for something to happen. In her mind, if something is not happening now, it is never going to happen.

My bipolar son is never on time. Why?

Children with bipolar disorder have difficulty seeing the world as a string of events that cause other events in an orderly fashion. Without a sense of how the past affects the future, your son may miss the regular passage of sequential events around him, which the rest of us use to keep track of what time it is. When the events around him seem to happen at random, it makes it hard for your son to gauge the passage of time. Also, when he is doing something absorbing, the time just seems to slip away. Failing to be aware of the time leads to the development of undesirable habits like lateness. I once did a survey of bipolar children and adults, asking when they would start getting ready for an appointment at six o'clock in the evening. Most of them answered, "Six o'clock," without thinking of the time necessary to stop what they were doing, get ready to go out, and travel to their destination.

Why is my daughter so negative about her future?

Inside your bipolar daughter's mind, the same difficulty with cause, effect, and stepwise thinking that makes bipolar children impatient and give up also makes it hard for her to visualize or predict what will happen in her future. If she feels that she is unsuccessful, she assumes that the situation is going to stay that way because she is unable to visualize how she could succeed. In her mind it seems like, "If something unpleasant is happening now, it's going to continue happening forever."

Q Why can't my bipolar child be more independent? I want him to be a self-starter.

Bipolar disorder makes it hard for your son to visualize which step should come after the next. Therefore, it is hard for him to plan, execute, and finish projects and assignments. From the outside, this looks like poor organization and an inability to get started without parents' assistance.

You can help your son by making a schedule to serve as an external framework for linear planning. This could include times for getting home from school, having a snack, starting homework, eating dinner, finishing homework, watching a television show, and going to bed. On weekends, it could establish times to wake up, eat breakfast, do chores, and have lunch. This structure can help him become more organized.

Q Why can't my bipolar son learn from his past experience? We punish him, but it doesn't help.

Difficulty with stepwise thinking makes it hard to connect cause with effect. For example, I remember a mother who had sent her child to his room on four consecutive days for playing with a delicate glass vase. For most children, this would teach them that playing with the vase leads to punishment and they would leave the glassware alone in the future. However, on the fifth day, the bipolar child played with the vase again and finally broke it. When his mother became upset, the only reason he could deduce was that she was in a bad mood that day. He was not able to connect the cause (playing with the vase) with the effect (his mother being upset and sending him to his room) in order to modify his own behavior.

In this case, the easiest strategy would have been to lock up the vase where her child could not get it, rather than relying on him to figure out that he was not supposed to touch it.

Why does my son stay out so late? He knows he'll get in trouble.

Your son has a hard time visualizing what lies in store for him after he gets home late because bipolar disorder causes him problems with linear, stepwise thinking about cause and effect. He can think about what's going on now, but it is difficult for him to anticipate what getting in trouble will be like until it is happening. In addition, some degree of grandiosity may be at work here, convincing him that, because he is special, the rules do not apply to him.

How does information processing affect my child in school?

Bipolar children's deficits in linear information processing often cause poor performance in school courses that rely heavily on linear, stepwise thinking, like algebra, physics, and chemistry. However, creative and verbal skills are not so dependent on linear, stepwise information-processing skills and bipolar children can often shine in these subjects.

What makes it so hard for my bipolar child to read?

In every sentence we read, we are always remembering the last few words we read and imagining what words we will read next. This element of cause and effect gives us a sense of where the story has been and where it is going. Bipolar children, even older ones, may not know what to look for to establish the who, what, and why of the story. Without a good sense of cause and effect, their reading does not make sense and, when they try to recall the details of the story, they cannot make sense of them.

My daughter did well in math until she had to take algebra. Why is that hard for bipolar children?

Your daughter and a lot of other bipolar children have difficulty with the linear, stepwise thinking that is required in much of mathematics. The mechanics of algebra, where symbols are used to stand for other symbols like numbers or equations, requires more linear, stepwise thinking than simpler math, which makes it just that much harder for bipolar children.

My bipolar daughter is so discouraged at school. She thinks she can't do anything well. Help!

Bipolar brain changes can make it difficult or impossible to succeed in highly linear school classes, and otherwise bright, creative children are made to feel that they are failures. The solution to this problem is for your daughter to practice being successful in the activities that she can do best. Introduce her to activities involving animals, acting, cinematography, cheerleading, choir, computer graphics, dance, ecology, fund-raising, musicals, or sculpture. When your daughter has a track record of consistent success, it will be easier for her to imagine how things can change for the better.

How can I help my son have a better attitude and develop better problem-solving abilities?

Help your child practice problem-solving in nonlinear activities that suit his talents and abilities. Help your child get experience in whatever hobby he shows interest in—whether it's camping, choir, ceramics, computer design, debate, illustration, maps, nature, photography, or other activities. As your child develops techniques for successful problem-solving in these activities, he will find it easier to visualize solutions in other, more linear, stepwise activities.

OVERTHINKING

Bipolar children tend to think too much and carry their assumptions and conclusions far beyond what is justified by the information they possess.

Why does the slightest problem always seem like a disaster to my bipolar son?

When you and I think, our thoughts go a few steps forward and stop for lack of information. If the problem is, "I forgot to bring home the English assignment," then we think, "So I better call somebody and get it," and our thought process stops there.

Overthinking changes the cognitive landscape. For example, if a bipolar girl starts thinking, "I forgot to bring home the English assignment," her next thoughts might be, "So I won't be able to do the assignment. But if I can't do my assignment, I might flunk English. And if I flunk English, I won't be able to get into a good journalism school. And if I can't get into a good journalism school, I won't be able to live my dream of being a journalist. And if I can't be a journalist, my life will have no meaning. So what's the point? My life is doomed anyway." In this exaggerated way of thinking, "I forgot to bring home the English assignment" means "My life will have no meaning, so what's the point?"

Why doesn't my bipolar girl think things through logically?

Overthinking trumps logic every time. One bipolar girl told me, "If I send one hundred dollars to a charity supported by a movie star, then the movie star might see it, and then she might call me up, and when she talks to me she will like me, and when she likes me she will want to help me out, and with her help, I'll be a movie star just like her." To our eyes, the end of this overthought story has nothing to do with the beginning. However, it appeared to the bipolar girl that if she just sent in a lot of money, she could start looking for a dress to wear to the Academy Awards.

INTRUSIVE THOUGHTS

Bipolar children's attention is easily captured by any strong thoughts or stimuli. If your child is trying to work on a math problem, a loud noise can invade your child's mind and knock out all the thoughts about math. Then your child must start all over again. If your child is happy, an unhappy thought can come into your child's mind and knock out the happy thought, making the child suddenly tearful. Unwanted thoughts can keep bombarding your child's mind over and over like a broken record. These repeating thoughts that children cannot keep out of their minds are called intrusive thoughts.

What causes my bipolar son to have attention problems and thinking difficulties?

Your son's dysfunctional brain cells affect his thought processing. Bipolar disorder makes it hard for your son to keep thoughts in his mind and hold them there. At the same time, it is hard for him to keep unwanted thoughts out of his mind. This means that any strong, irrelevant, distracting thought or emotion can enter his mind and drive out the thought that is there. For example, in school, distracting thoughts will drive out lectures and reading assignments so quickly that they do not even get a chance to register in your son's memory. Later, when he searches his memory for this information to do homework or take a test, it will not be there. This memory failure also explains the times he misses appointments, deadlines, and test dates, and why his books, personal items, and school assignments get misplaced and lost.

Because he cannot hold thoughts in his mind, it is hard for your son to concentrate, follow conversations, and keep to the point, and he may tend to blurt out comments and interrupt others when they are speaking. Because he cannot remember experiences and their consequences, he will have difficulty recalling what he has learned, difficulty learning from past events, and difficulty seeing the process of cause and effect in his life.

What causes intrusive thoughts in my twin bipolar sons?

This problem results from a failure of the "mental gate" that keeps important thoughts in and unwanted thoughts out of the mind. Medications can help eliminate intrusive thoughts by making each of your sons' "mental gate" work the way it is supposed to.

Why does my bipolar daughter get stuck on certain ideas and activities?

Sometimes strong distracting thoughts enter your daughter's mind, capture her attention, and get stuck there, resulting in obsessive thinking, repetitive behavior patterns, and difficulty changing bad habits. Your daughter becomes vulnerable to strong emotions, which can appear suddenly in her mind and stay there until they are suddenly knocked out by another distraction.

My bipolar depressed daughter always thinks the worst about herself and everything around her. Where did she get this bad self-image?

This situation may be caused by intrusive thoughts, not a learned self-image. When your daughter is depressed, she cannot control which thoughts come into her mind. Gradually, the most awful negative thoughts take over her consciousness, because they are so strong that they can push the other, happier thoughts out of her mind. These are intrusive thoughts. When your daughter tries to pay attention in class, intrusive thoughts are there, distracting and demoralizing her. When she tries to go to sleep, she is tortured by repeating negative thoughts. The solution is to ask your psychiatrist to adjust her medications to reduce intrusive thoughts and this situation should improve.

GRANDIOSITY

Grandiosity is the belief that you are someone very special without evidence to that effect. Grandiose children believe that rules do not apply to them, that they can have whatever they want, that they can do whatever they want, and that their welfare and convenience come before everyone else's. Grandiose children think that they are more powerful, more talented, and more deserving of attention than anyone else.

As one young bipolar child described it, "It's all about MEEEE!"

What are some simple examples of grandiosity that I might see in my daughter?

Always having to be right, hogging the conversation, pushing ahead of others in line, hurting others' feelings, speeding, cheating, lying, and stealing are all messages that your child thinks she is better than everybody else and is not held accountable to the usual rules of society.

My bipolar daughter spends so much time helping her friends with their homework that she can't get her own homework done. Then they get good grades and she gets bad grades. Why?

In addition to having a genuine wish to help others, showing that you know more than your friends provides an ego boost that feeds right into a grandiose sense of oneself. Unfortunately, enhancing a grandiose view of herself does not help your daughter do well in school, develop her creative talents, learn how to have mature relationships, or plan for the future. Point out to her that, in exchange for looking clever to her friends, she is cheating herself out of what she needs to succeed. She can help her friends *after* she finishes with her schoolwork, if she has the time and inclination.

Q My bipolar manic child always wants the best
of everything. What is she thinking?

This is grandiosity again. If you think you are better than anyone else, it makes
sense that you should only have the best, no matter what the cost to others.
This grandiosity is a part of impulsive spending, demanding gifts that parents refuse, and wanting to own everything that catches her fancy. Do not
be surprised if your daughter becomes indignant and angry when you tell
her that she cannot have anything she wants, any time she wants it.

Q My mother caught me shoplifting and she's
making a big fuss. She doesn't know that
I do it all the time. I feel really guilty
about it, but I can't seem to help myself.

Shoplifting is usually driven by anger, shame, and grandiosity. If you are angry, you may steal small items to show your disdain for the world in general. When you feel guilty, you may openly steal in a backward attempt to get
punished for your shortcomings. However it happens, grandiosity plays a
role in making you feel that you can do the things that everyone else is pro-
hibited from doing. If you cannot sort this out by yourself, ask for help
from your parents, therapist, or physician.

Q My bipolar son says he can't do schoolwork
because he is too perfectionistic. How
can this be true?

After putting projects off to the last moment, imagining how wonderful his
work will be, and making a big production out of the task, your son may
realize that the final product will be an embarrassment. Your son may have
difficulty completing projects anyway, because of the effects of bipolar disorder, and perfectionism is one way of rationalizing this.

AN EXAMPLE OF GRANDIOSITY

Grandiosity can be very subtle and pervasive. For example, the parents of one of my patients told their daughter that they would buy her an expensive dress if she made good grades and stayed out of trouble. They hoped that her behavior would improve if she had a concrete goal on which to focus. Although she continued making bad grades and breaking the rules, she was sure that she would get the dress anyway. She persisted in this belief even when her parents and I told her frankly that she would not receive the dress because she had not fulfilled her part of the deal. Her response was, "They *have* to give me the dress. They *have* to." This response seems illogical to those without bipolar disorder but seemed perfectly reasonable to her. In her mind, she was special and she could break the rules without consequence.

This example seems less trivial when you realize that this girl was also thinking that she could flunk high school and still graduate, that she could drive perfectly well while drunk, that it was okay for her to lie to get out of trouble, that she could live the rest of her life by sponging off her family, and that she could hurt and alienate her family and friends without culpability. She believed that, because of her specialness, she would not have to face the negative consequences of her actions.

LEAKY INTERPERSONAL BOUNDARIES

Interpersonal boundaries refer to the imaginary border where one person stops and another begins. When interpersonal boundaries are strong, children have a good idea of who they are and how they are different from others. However, if a bipolar child has leaky boundaries, it can become hard to tell where he or she stops and other people begin.

What do interpersonal boundaries have to do with my bipolar son?

Individuals with bipolar disorder often have leaky interpersonal boundaries, so that if they see a sad person, they feel sad, or if they hear about a person in pain, they feel the pain as if it were happening to them. Leaky boundaries can make your son too vulnerable to other people's emotions and too dependent on their thoughts and opinions.

Why is my daughter still crying about a tragedy that happened weeks ago in another country?

Bipolar disorder can make your daughter's interpersonal boundaries so weak that the pain and misfortune that is happening to other people feels like it is happening to her. Your daughter cannot keep the sense of other people's pain out of her mind, even if it is irrelevant to her life.

Why does my daughter care so much about what everybody else thinks?

It sounds strange, but when your daughter has leaky boundaries, it is hard for her to tell the difference between her thoughts and other people's thoughts. It may seem to your daughter that she has to ask other people's opinions in order to see how *she* feels about herself. Encourage her to be independent and to trust her own opinions of herself.

How did my bipolar son get so preoccupied with whether people like him or not?

All children start with immature, leaky interpersonal boundaries, unable to distinguish their own thoughts and feelings from those of their mother. Young children look for their mothers' reactions to see whether they are doing the right thing. As children grow older, their interpersonal boundaries usually grow stronger, and older children develop their own identity, unique and separate from others. They learn to look inside themselves to see whether they are doing the right thing or not. However, many bipolar children never outgrow these immature leaky boundaries. They have difficulty seeing themselves as unique, separate individuals, and they continue the childish habit of watching others' reactions to see if they are doing the

SOME THINGS THAT YOUR BIPOLAR CHILD MAY HAVE DIFFICULTY UNDERSTANDING

1. Change takes time. Do not assume that you will never get what you want just because you do not have it now. Be patient.
2. Events are governed by cause and effect. Look at what has happened in the past to predict what will happen to you now.
3. Do not overthink the events in your life or try to predict the future. Draw your best conclusions and then stop.
4. Just because you are having unhappy thoughts does not mean you have to be unhappy.
5. You will always have disappointments and you will have to do things you do not want to do, just like everyone else.

right thing. This excessive concern about what others think can become extreme or obsessive and it can affect your son's ability to make good decisions.

For example, I sat down one day with a young bipolar girl who was failing math. I suggested homework and note-taking strategies, offered to help her get tutoring, and tried to encourage her to study harder, but she was not impressed. "I know I will get a good grade in math," she told me, "because I'm sure the teacher likes me." It was hard for her to understand that mathematics grades depend upon quiz and test scores, not on whether the teacher likes her.

9.

HELPING YOUR
BIPOLAR CHILD
SUCCEED IN SCHOOL

As it is now, school programs are not built around the strengths of bipolar children, and most schools require bipolar children to do things they just cannot do well. Unfortunately, grade schools and high schools still focus primarily on topics that require too much linear, stepwise thinking like algebra, precalculus, physics, chemistry, foreign languages, and spelling. As explained in Chapter 8, the brain changes that are caused by bipolar disorder can make these classes a barrier to bipolar children.

On the other hand, bipolar children's brains are often better equipped to handle subjects like art, art history, chorale, cinematography, computer design, computer graphics, creative writing, drafting, drama, music, musical theater, politics, photography, public speaking, and stagecraft. These subject areas can form the basis for college performance and successful future careers for bipolar children, who need grade school and high school education and encouragement in such subjects to prepare them for successful lives. In my opinion, schools should allow bipolar children to specialize in the areas where they can excel.

Q What's the most important thing I can do to
     help my bipolar son do better in school?

The most important thing is to see that his medical treatment and psychotherapy are optimized and that he has as few bipolar symptoms as possible.
More than 70 percent of individuals with untreated bipolar disorder have
school or job problems. After receiving appropriate treatment, this figure decreases significantly.

Q Why does my son get in trouble at school,
     and where do we start to prevent it?

Even before his bipolar disorder began to be treated, your son began to develop habits to try to cope with his bipolar symptoms. These may include
trying to ignore his problems, using humor or irritability to defend against
tasks that seem too difficult, lying, or using anger to get what he wants. Your
son cannot begin to work on decreasing these habits until his dysfunctional
brain cells are working properly, so first start by getting your son's medications and therapy in order.

Q My school's teachers and counselor told me
     that my son doesn't have bipolar disorder.
     They say his problem is poor self-esteem,
     a bad attitude, poor social skills, and
     behavioral problems. They imply that
     it is our fault and they want us to stop
     his medications. Do you have any
     suggestions?

It may not occur to your school staff that poor self-esteem, a bad attitude,
poor social skills, and irritability can be *symptoms* of bipolar disorder. Do

not stop your child's medications on their recommendation; this is a decision for you and your child's psychiatrist to make. When your son's medications and therapy are optimized, and stress is under control, the school staff is likely to see improvement in all these areas. It may also help them if you can give them something to read about bipolar disorder, so that they can understand it better.

HELP YOUR CHILD WITH HOMEWORK AND STUDYING

Doing homework is one of the biggest problems bipolar children face. Bipolar disorder makes it difficult to start projects, and bipolar children can spend hours getting ready or fooling around before they even begin to do their homework. If they wait until it is too late in the evening, they may end up working through the night and missing the sleep that is so essential for their health. For this reason, I recommend that homework be put on a schedule so that it starts and stops at the same time every day. If your child gets through his or her assignments early, there is always extra reviewing or extra-credit work that can be done. When your child becomes accustomed to spending a specified time every day doing schoolwork, it will be easier for him or her to keep up in school and be prepared for quizzes and tests.

What does my son need to do to get good grades?

The prescription for good grades is to do the homework and reading nightly, ask the teacher questions in class, and study before examinations. Older children should study at least four hours before each test.

What about tutors? Are they any help for school?

If you can find a tutor who can work effectively with your bipolar child, grab that person quick before someone else does. Many tutors know what works to motivate children, and they may be able to get the best from your child.

Q I heard that my school would give my bipolar daughter special accommodations. Is this true?

Many children I treat receive special help from their school in the form of special accommodations. Your daughter may get the opportunity to take un-timed tests, the right to preferential seating near the front of the class, and the right to take tests in a quiet environment without distractions. Other kinds of accommodations are also possible, depending on your school and the community. You can ask your school principal, counselor, tutor, or doctor for help. Your daughter's psychiatrist may simply have to write a note re-questing and justifying specific accommodations based on your daughter's bipolar diagnosis.

Q What do you suggest for my daughter? She says she can't understand her teacher's assignments.

Tell her to sit in the front of the class, watch the teacher's mouth when he or she is giving out assignments, write them down, and then ask the teacher to check that what your daughter wrote down is correct.

Q My son forgets to bring home his assignments and books. We need a solution.

Ask your son's teachers if they will post each day's assignments on the school's Internet page. This is standard practice in many schools already. If your son forgets to bring home the right books, get your child a bigger book bag so he can carry all his books with him all the time.

My son says he's so tired and overwhelmed after school that he just can't pick up a schoolbook.

Bipolar depression causes a kind of heavy "lead pipe" fatigue that overlaps poor motivation and makes everything seem like a chore. If your son comes home late from school, has sports practice, or does not start his homework until after dinner, the amount of effort it takes to do schoolwork can feel intolerable. That is why I recommend that all bipolar children start their homework as soon as they arrive home and review it with their parents before starting any other activities.

Why does my bipolar son get so worked up about examinations? He can't study that way, and fails.

The impending threat of tests causes stress that can fuel anxiety and panic. Eventually, panic can become a habitual response to performance anxiety. However, if your son has kept up in class and spent time every day studying and reviewing the material, he will probably be able to do well on the test and feel less stressed out.

How else can I help my son get the grades he is capable of?

This is where some negotiating skills pay off. Bipolar children need a tangible target to shoot for. If your son has some career, school, or future dream that will be unattainable without good grades in school, you can point this out to him. I once motivated a brilliant bipolar girl who turned her high school career around when she found out what grades she would need to attend photography school.

If this fails, then find out what your child wants and offer it to him if he makes a certain grade point average. It could be a short trip, a musical instrument, a computer, or sports equipment that he would not get otherwise. Give him specific numbers to attain, such as a 3.1 grade point average, or five As and two Bs. Bipolar children can understand working in their own self-interest better than they can stay focused on some abstract goal like being a good student. Then, offer an additional reward for doing even better the next semester.

Q **I feel like a hypocrite telling my son to study when I never studied in high school. High school is supposed to be fun.**

If you look around this modern world, you will see that everything is tougher than when you were in school and there is a lot more to learn. If your bipolar son is not able to get through high school with good credentials, then he will be cut off from the best colleges and jobs, not just because he does not have the grades, but also because he never learned the discipline and self-sacrifice necessary to succeed in the real world. The competition is fierce out there and your bipolar son is starting at a disadvantage. He cannot afford to slack off and you cannot afford to let him.

Q **What is your experience using school counselors as psychotherapists for bipolar children?**

It all depends on the counselor. Some are great therapists and some are not so good. You will have to check out your school counselor's knowledge and experience with bipolar disorder and make your own decision. Their services are usually free.

STUDY TIPS AND HABITS

Bipolar children need all the strategies and tricks possible to help give them an edge in their schoolwork.

Q Does my son really need a desk to study and do homework?

Yes. Your child needs a place where he can put his books and papers out without running into clutter or being disturbed by others. His study place should have good light and be free from distractions like television, radio, telephone, or video games in the background. The desk need not be fancy; resin or unfinished wooden desks are available inexpensively and they serve quite well.

Q What is the one condition when my daughter shouldn't have a private desk?

Your daughter should not have a private desk if she can't do her work alone. If your bipolar daughter needs supervision to keep studying, the kitchen or dining room table may provide enough visibility so you or another family member can put her back on course when she becomes distracted. I know of one family whose bipolar daughter does her homework on a very visible table at her father's office. With so many people around, it is hard for her to stop working and start playing around.

Q Do you have suggestions on how my daughter can get organized, remember assignments, and study for tests?

File cards provide a concrete, nonlinear way to organize information that suits bipolar children with short attention spans. Start by having your daughter write down assignments on a card and cross off each one when it is done. When a card gets full, start another. This way, nothing gets overlooked. When studying for a test, have her jot down short reminders of concepts and terms she needs to learn on separate file cards. Then have her go through each card with you and explain each concept and term from memory. If one eludes explanation, have your child go back to her book and notes until the material is clear and she can explain it from memory.

How much note taking should I do in class?
If I write too much I can't follow the
teacher and sometimes I can't even read
my notes later on.

Note taking is a perennial problem. If you have some system that works for you, keep it up. If not, consider this. You cannot write down everything. Your job is to sift through the classroom material to find the important facts and relationships. I suggest that you look at the classroom as a source of test material. Try to write down the material you think you will be asked on quizzes and examinations. This exercise forces you to think about the meaning and organization of what you are learning. Then when you are studying, you will focus on the meat of the subject and avoid becoming distracted.

My son says his friend listens to his
headphones while studying. Isn't this
more distracting?

Actually, some bipolar children study better with music or the radio playing because it helps them block out other distracting stimuli. It is worth a try to see if your child studies better that way or not.

What's the biggest hurdle for bipolar
students like me working on
compositions and papers?

There is no doubt that waiting until the last moment will torpedo your best writing efforts. If you can keep to your schedule and work on your projects a few minutes every day, you will lower your stress level and should get better grades. Tell your parents about your deadlines and help them encourage you to do the necessary work before the deadline.

10.

TEENS TALK ABOUT
BIPOLAR DISORDER

. . . .

Bipolar disorder presents unique challenges to adolescents. Difficulties with impaired concentration, fatigue, mood swings, depression, or sleeping problems can make everything seem more difficult. In addition, teenage bipolar disorder brings its own set of questions and problems to solve.

How can you be sure I have bipolar disorder? I don't want to get treatment if I don't have to.

The best way to be sure is to review the diagnostic criteria in Chapter 2 and decide how much these symptoms are interfering with your performance in schoolwork and in your relationships with family and other teens. On the other hand, if you have begun treatment and it is helping you in these and other areas of your life, this is a strong argument for continuing bipolar treatment. Remember, medical treatment is not about pride or principle or making a statement about yourself; it is about helping you do your best and getting what you want in life.

I don't like it when my therapist keeps
reminding me that I have bipolar disorder
all the time. I'd prefer to forget about it.

When you try to forget that you have a problem, you are avoiding the truth
and creating a fantasy that things are different than they really are. Unfortunately, avoidance and fantasy are two of the major stumbling blocks that
keep adolescents with bipolar disorder from succeeding in life. Don't let your
ego get the best of you. Accept the fact that you are not perfect and, like
everyone else you know, you have some problems to work on.

I don't like the idea of medications. Aren't
they unnatural?

The purpose of using medications is to help return you to your most natural self, the way you would have been if you had never developed bipolar
disorder. Without medications, your bipolar disorder forces you to think,
feel, and act in ways that are unnatural for you. Mood stabilizers can help
you become yourself.

Why won't my doctor give me an anxiety
medication? My friend tried Valium and
Xanax and said they made him feel better.

Sedatives like Valium and Xanax are best used for pure anxiety disorders.
They are addictive, change natural sleep patterns, promote irritability, and
interfere with learning. Mood stabilizers are used to treat anxiety in bipolar
disorder, and they have none of these undesirable side effects.

Why do I feel sleepy all day? Everybody in school laughs at me because I keep falling asleep.

Daytime sleepiness, inability to get up in the morning, and fatigue are directly caused by bipolar depression. Your adolescent body loses track of time and tries to make you sleep during the day and be awake late at night. To combat this problem, start by going to bed earlier. Make sure you go to bed and get up at regular times every day. This will help your body learn when it is time to sleep and when it is time to be awake. If you feel that you need more help to sleep, consider asking your doctor to strengthen your mood-stabilizing medication(s). This treats the heart of the problem, unlike sleeping pills, which just knock you out.

How can my doctor strengthen my bipolar medications?

Your doctor can raise the dose of the mood stabilizer(s) you are currently taking, add a low dose of another mood stabilizer, or add another kind of medication to your regimen. The first two options are best, because mood stabilizers are the major medications that can help return you to your most natural self.

I'm tortured with thoughts all day at school. What can keep bad thoughts out of my head?

Distracting thoughts can make adolescent life miserable, and reducing intrusive, unwanted thoughts is what mood stabilizers do best. They improve your ability to keep good thoughts *in* your conscious mind and to keep bad, distracting thoughts *out* of your mind, so you can get on with your life.

Q Which mood stabilizer is best for my
    weight problem?

Right now, it appears that lamotrigine and carbamazepine have the least potential for weight gain, with lithium salt in the middle and valproate showing the greatest potential for weight gain. Topiramate helps many teens lose weight, but it is not the best treatment for bipolar disorder.

Q Can I drink grapefruit juice? Other girls are
    losing weight on the "grapefruit diet."

Eating grapefruit or drinking grapefruit juice can lower the blood levels of your mood stabilizer medications by increasing digestive enzymes. This can make it seem that your bipolar symptoms are worsening when it is really just grapefruit keeping your medicine from getting to your body. Stay away from grapefruit and eat apples, apricots, grapes, peaches, plums, and other raw fruits instead. Check with your doctor for more dietary information.

Q I heard on the news that antidepressants make
    teens depressed and suicidal. Is this true?

Antidepressants can make adolescents *with bipolar disorder* feel depressed and suicidal. This is one reason why doctors should never give antidepressants to anyone who has bipolar disorder.

Q Every teen I know has thought of suicide
    at some time or other. How do I know
    if my suicidal thoughts are a serious
    problem or not?

Here are some questions to help you understand how serious your thoughts are:

- Do you have vague thoughts about death,
  OR do you have a specific plan in mind to kill yourself?
- Do you think about suicide every so often,
  OR many times per day?
- Are you taking your bipolar medicine regularly,
  OR have you reduced or stopped your dose?
- Are you using the support of friends, relatives, psychiatrist, and therapist,
  OR are you trying to handle bipolar problems on your own?
- Do you have loved ones who would be heartbroken by your death,
  OR are you mainly thinking of yourself right now?
- Is your judgment good and your thoughts clear,
  OR are you using alcohol or other drugs that could cloud your judgment?
- Are you a spiritual person who believes it is wrong to kill yourself,
  OR do you not care much about spiritual things?

If you endorse any of the "OR" answers, discuss them with your psychiatrist and therapist.

FAMILY, SCHOOL, AND THE INTERNET

As a teen, you are faced with life challenges at home, in school, and in your personal life. With a little help, you can keep bipolar disorder from interfering with your success in these important areas.

What can I say to my parents after I get angry and tell them that I hate them?

All you can do is apologize later and tell your parents that you love them. If these anger episodes are interfering with your life, tell your doctor and therapist that you want to make them stop.

Q My grandmother had recurrent depression. Could this have been undiagnosed bipolar disorder?

Some doctors think that depression that recurs every year at the same time is really bipolar depression. Because bipolar disorder runs in families, it is certainly possible that your grandmother was bipolar.

Q My father is so unreasonable. I don't know if I can take much more. Help!

It is common for there to be some friction between adolescents and parents. Parents are not prepared for the changes that come with your physical and mental maturity, and bipolar disorder can make things more difficult by decreasing your patience and increasing your irritability. However, no matter how unreasonable your parents are, you still have to deal with them, and they will continue to control your life until you are eighteen years old. On the other hand, you are bound to find other very unreasonable people during the course of your life that you will also have to deal with. Try to use this time to build up your best skills at negotiating, devising compromises, putting up with annoying personality traits, and making the best out of your situation. It will serve you well for the rest of your life.

Q Why do my parents give me chores like running errands, yard work, and housework? Other kids don't have to do this stuff and they have their freedom.

Every family is different in what they require from their children. They assign chores; set expectations for school, sports, or family activities; or have no expectations whatsoever. Everyone has a different set of adolescent responsibilities, just like they will have different opportunities later in life. Bipolar disorder can make chores seem like they take forever, but they do not. If you

focus on increasing your efficiency and avoiding distractions and procrastination, you will finish your chores as fast as possible and you may still have
some free time left.

My younger sister is smarter than me, and she takes every opportunity to embarrass me in front of my parents and my friends. Why is she doing this to me?

Sometimes bipolar children require extra care, and parents spend lots of
time taking them to doctors, therapists, and so forth. Siblings may be jealous
of this extra parental attention and feel that they have to try harder to get
their parents' attention and approval. Also, she may look up to you and do
her best to make herself look good in front of you. I am sure you do not appreciate your sister's attempts to show how important she is, but it demon-
strates that she cares about what you think; uncaring sisters would just
ignore you altogether.

If you try taking more time to get to know your sister and do more
things with her, her jealousy may melt away. And remember, although she
may do better than you in school, it does not necessarily mean she is
smarter than you. If you do not know it already, you may discover that you
have special talents and abilities that allow you to do wonderful things that
your sister cannot do.

Why does everybody make such a big deal out of school? I think it is stupid.

Many bipolar teens tell me they do not consider school important, but it is
really very important to you. To be able to use and enjoy your own personal
strengths, talents, and abilities in your adult life, you must first pass through
a maze of national educational requirements. At the same time, you must get
an educational foundation strong enough to support your daily adult life in
this competitive world.

I'm rotten at composition. Do you have any suggestions for writing papers?

Writing linear and logical compositions, using step-by-step methods, poses a big challenge for many bipolar teens (see Chapter 8). However, papers can be constructed using a less-linear approach. Start by using file cards to keep track of the material for your paper. Most papers are based on quotations and ideas from other sources. Look for quotes on your topic on the Internet or in the library, and write each one on a blank file card. When you have enough material, spread everything out on the floor, and put the file cards together in an order that tells a story. Try to let the quotations suggest their own order. For example, some ideas clearly have to come first, and then others, while some will not be used at all. Then, with your file cards arranged in a stack, go through them one by one, using each quotation as the basis of a point in your paper. The result will be well organized, show good use of resources, and be likely to garner a good grade.

Why do I always wait till the last minute to do my schoolwork?

Bipolar disorder usually causes problems with procrastination. I remember one bipolar adolescent who explained it to me this way:

> I always wait till the last minute to start anything important. Then the fear of embarrassment and failure pushes me so hard that I *have* to do the project. I try and try to start earlier, but I never can. If I *am* able to work on a project, then it's hard to finish it. I have lots of projects sitting around, almost done, but I just can't finish them up unless there is an emergency.

Bipolar disorder causes problems starting and finishing projects but, if you work hard on your schedule, you can train yourself to spend a block of time doing your assignments every day. Once you have dedicated this time solely to doing assignments, it will be easier to start assignments earlier and work on them until they are completed. You can break out of this prison of procrastination. Other teens have done it and you can, too.

I don't really care about school. I have more fun in sports.

You do not care now, but your future spouse, children, grandchildren, and friends will all care if you do not have a good, stable career when you are older. The key to getting what you want later in life is doing your best in school now. Get enough exercise to ensure that you are healthy, but make learning your priority.

Can't I get a fast track to college with a football or baseball scholarship?

Yes, but it is a risky bet. Our educational pathway is built around academic success. It is better if you find school subjects where you can excel, study, and get good grades in them.

I want to use the Internet to make new friends, but my parents object. What do you think?

Internet friends and e-mail pals are good to have as long as you *never* try to meet them in person. You can use the Internet as a way to interact with people in other countries and other cultures; this is a broadening experience. However, you cannot find out enough about anyone over the Internet to ensure that direct contact will be safe. If you cannot abide by this restriction, then you should not use the Internet to make new friends.

Q There is someone who has become very pushy, sending me e-mails, calling, and texting me all the time. How can I discourage this person?

If someone is taking up too much of your time, distracting you at home or school, stirring up gossip, or being secretive or sexual in any way, stop all your communications with them. Tell them once that you are breaking off contact, then do not read or reply to their messages. If necessary, be prepared to change your e-mail address. There are too many interesting, rewarding people in the world to bother with troublemakers.

Q How much should I reveal about myself on the Internet?

Never reveal anything about yourself on the Internet. The Internet is a great place to learn about others without revealing any personal information of your own. Do not be tempted to post anything inflammatory on the Internet that could later be traced to you. Do not ever give out your real name, address, telephone number, or details about your life that anybody else could identify. Remember that there are malevolent characters on the Web looking for a chance to annoy, worry, harass, disturb, stalk, rob (especially credit information), and do both personal and bodily harm to whomever leaves themselves unprotected. You do not need to become mysterious or coy or make up an alter ego. Just keep your private details to yourself. Privacy is becoming increasingly rare nowadays, so protect yours whenever you can.

Q Is there any way I can talk to other teenagers who also have bipolar disorder?

Look in Chapter 12 to find bipolar blogs, support groups, bulletin boards, and other gathering places for bipolar teens. You can talk as much as you want in these venues without stigma or embarrassment. You can get support from other adolescents, learn their coping strategies, and help other bipolar teens.

FRIENDS AND RELATIONSHIPS

Social life is an important part of being a teen. Relationships help you build social skills, learn how to choose friends and be a friend, and prepare for married and family life later on. Unfortunately, bipolar disorder sometimes makes it hard to meet people, make friends, and keep them.

Why am I so painfully shy? I never talk at school and I find it hard to make friends.

Bipolar disorder, particularly bipolar depression, often brings periods of shyness, withdrawal, and social isolation. If this happens too much during the teen years, you may never get enough practice socializing to feel at ease around strangers. Eventually, avoiding others can become a habit.

I really don't like meeting new people. Do I have to go out?

It would be nice if friends just popped up out of the ground like wildflowers, but friends need to be cultivated. Show up at group activities where you will be around familiar teens and some new faces as well. When you meet people you would like as friends, call or text them to say hi. It is well worth the effort when you find other people you enjoy being around.

Everybody says "Just go up and say hello to someone," but I can't make conversation. Help!

The problem is not saying hello. The difficulty comes in knowing what to say after hello. This is my plan. First, ask the other teen what they are interested in. Say, "So, what kind of things do you like to do?" or "Are you interested in (sports, current events, music, and so forth)?" Whatever they mention, say "Tell me more about that." You do not have to know anything about their interests; in fact, it is better if you do not. Just practice being a good listener. It's fun to learn about other people and what they think and do. If you are having fun, let the other person talk to *you*. They will love you for it. If you find that you are just not having fun with this person, then bail. There are plenty of other people to meet, now that you know what to do.

What do I do if I'm out with my friend and there's a silence during a conversation?

Silences are natural and they give you a chance to enjoy being with your friend without distractions. You are not an entertainer or a party host and it is not your job to keep conversations moving. Just let your interactions play out naturally and enjoy them as they unfold. In all your interactions, just be yourself. If you can concentrate on acting naturally, you will find friends who like you for the person you really are.

Why is it that whenever I'm with people, all I can think about is pleasing them?

If you like people and want them to like you, it seems reasonable to try to please them. However, good friends want to be with you because they like who you are, not because you will do things for them. Ultimately, acting naturally will make good friends like you better.

I'm a social butterfly, but after a while, my new friends always start to avoid me. Why?

You may be a glib and magnetic conversationalist but, if you do not know when to stop, you may eventually seem intrusive and annoying. This excess energy can alienate other teens and make them want to avoid you. If you try hard and are unable to moderate hyperactivity, loudness, interruptions, talking too much, and other bipolar symptoms, discuss the problem with your doctor and therapist.

I'm always calling and giving people I like cards and little presents, but they don't respond.

It may be that you are trying too hard. Other teens will not like it if you seem too pushy, and they will naturally try to draw away. Besides, people need some time away from you so they can appreciate how much they like being with you.

Other teens tell me I'm intense, but I don't want to be. What can I do?

People will think you are intense if you talk too much or get in their face. Even if you are feeling on edge, it does not have to rub off on your friends. Slow down. Talk less and listen more. Lighten up and put on a smile. This will make other adolescents feel more comfortable around you.

How can I increase my willpower so I am not so irritable? I'm pushing my friends away.

Willpower is not an effective way of combating bipolar irritability. If anger is interfering with your life, tell your psychiatrist to adjust your medications so you are not so angry, and ask your therapist to begin anger-management therapy. Get anger under control now, before you lose people that you care about.

Why can't I keep a secret? I always say
          whatever comes into my head.

Your friends will not want to confide in you if you tell their secrets to other
teens. Unfortunately, bipolar disorder often causes impulsive speech, where
ideas in your head come out before you can stop them. One temporary solution to this problem is to ask your friends not to tell you secrets. Work on
this impulsive problem in your therapy sessions and ask other teens in bipolar support groups how they handle it.

Should I tell my friends what goes on in my
          psychotherapy sessions?

In general, I think that what goes on in your therapy sessions is for you
alone. Even the best of adolescent friends can sometimes blab details that
you want kept confidential. Also, therapy may not work as well if you are
planning on sharing everything that happens with other people. We all tend
to censor ourselves or act differently when we have an audience. This can get
in the way of honesty in therapy sessions and in your own life. It may also blur
the boundaries between fact and fiction, reality and fantasy. I once worked
with a bipolar girl who spent all night on the telephone with a celebrity
friend after our sessions going over every detail that transpired. Those conversations did not help the therapy and may have delayed her progress.

Can everybody tell that I have bipolar
          disorder? I always think people will know.

No one can guess that you have bipolar disorder unless you give the secret
away. Others may notice that you are moody, tired, or hyperactive, but most
people do not know enough about bipolar disorder to put the clues together.

Whenever anyone asks me about myself, I can't help lying to make myself look better. What's happening?

Lying in an attempt to make yourself look better to others is very common in bipolar disorder and it can get you into big trouble if your lies are detected. Why do you think that you are not interesting enough on your own, without embellishing the details? Potential friends want to get to know you as you are, not some fantasy character you have created. If you make up lies to sound more important, you will get friends who like you only for the lies and not for yourself.

I'm a teenage bipolar girl. What's the best thing to do with a guy I really like?

One of the best things to do is to study together. You'll get some school-work done, and it is a good test of potential relationship material. If you can sit together studying with a guy for an hour without him being annoying, distracting, or immature, you might be a good pair.

My friends all tell me that this guy treats me badly, but I can't get him out of my mind. Help!

When you fantasize about a person, it is hard to let him go and difficult to see if he is treating you badly. It is hard to part with such a perfect fantasy person, and it feels like you would lose a part of yourself if the two of you were separated. Look inside yourself to find the strong, self-sufficient person who does not need a fantasy friend to hang on to. When you are able to think beyond this fantasy, you can reclaim your thoughts for yourself.

How can I keep from worrying about my girlfriend? I always think she's flirting with other guys. Is bipolar disorder related to pathological jealousy?

Every adolescent has feelings of jealousy at one time or another. However, if jealous thoughts are too severe, they can intrude on your life, making it hard for you to concentrate on schoolwork and difficult for you to fall asleep—not to mention destroying your relationships with others. See if you can put this person out of your mind for a while. You may have to draw back from the relationship if it is causing you problems. If you are unable to turn off your thoughts, then ask your psychiatrist to adjust your medications to help you reduce intrusive thoughts.

I'm a freshman, and a senior is trying to ask me out. Should I avoid him?

You must realize that there is a big gulf between you and this senior in both maturity and experience. This makes you vulnerable, and the impulsivity that goes with bipolar disorder makes you more vulnerable still.

If you choose to pursue this relationship, consider starting out seeing this senior while you are with your family. Have him over to family dinner, invite him to family functions, ask him to go with your family to church, and so on. This will help you learn a lot about him while you are on safe territory.

I suddenly realized I'm in love with someone at school. What should I do?

Love is not such a rare thing. Ask yourself, "Do I have the potential for a healthy, enjoyable relationship with this person?" You will be surprised how often the honest answer is "No." If that is the case, just enjoy the feeling and keep meeting new people until the relationship potential is there.

RULES FOR SAFE BIPOLAR DATING

Dating does not have to mean two people alone. You can always arrange to see people you like in a group or family situation, or in a public place. However you choose to see new people, take these precautions.

1. If at any time you feel that you are not being treated with respect, or feel uncomfortable with the situation, just make up some excuse and go home. There is no reason to waste your time if you are uncomfortable.
2. If you can drive conveniently, drive yourself. Otherwise, make sure you can always call your parents to come pick you up and take you home. It makes you too vulnerable if you have to depend on a stranger to take you home.
3. Don't mix alcohol or marijuana with dating; you need a clear head when you are out with others.
4. Don't *ever* go out or become romantic with teachers, coaches, counselors, doctors, therapists, relatives, or adults in general. The difference in power is too great to allow a natural, healthy relationship.

I've fallen in love with a teacher who's helping me after school. Is it okay to go over to her house?

It is not okay. Teachers, coaches, doctors, and therapists are not allowed to date the adolescents they help, for good reason. In addition to the age difference, there is a difference in power between the two of you that makes you vulnerable to being hurt.

GIRLS ONLY

Menstrual cycles can be challenging for bipolar girls, and your periods may seem much worse than your girlfriends'. Bipolar disorder can cause severe PMS that begins around the time of ovulation and lasts up to two weeks, until your period begins. On the days just before your period, your bipolar symptoms may worsen, leaving you with additional depression, anxiety, impulsivity, irritability, and anger.

Q One of my doctors said that antidepressants could treat PMS. Are they safe for my bipolar disorder?

Even small doses of antidepressants for a few days a month are enough to destabilize your bipolar disorder. Do not use antidepressants to treat PMS.

TEENS TALK ABOUT SEX

Bipolar disorder can cause adolescents' interest in sex to go way up or way down. It can stimulate unwanted sexual thoughts and behavior in teens who are not interested in or prepared for these experiences. We usually expect sexual interest to go down with bipolar depression and up with bipolar mania, but in mixed bipolar disorder, anything is possible.

Q My girlfriend is always pushing me to kiss and touch her. Is that the only reason she likes me?

That may not be the only reason your girlfriend likes you, but sex can often capture others' attention. If you do not want this kind of attention from your girlfriend, tell her so. If she is disappointed, she may act hurt, but you will find out once and for all whether she likes you for yourself or your body.

Q I'm very religious, but last weekend I acted real sexual with someone. What's going on?

Bipolar disorder can cause sexual behavior to occur suddenly at unexpected times even in teens who do not want to be sexual. As an adolescent, you may not have much experience dealing with such strong sexual impulses, and it may be difficult to control them.

When is bipolar disorder most likely to cause me to act sexual with someone?

Impulsive sexuality is much more likely if you are drinking or smoking marijuana, which is one reason I advise against using these when you are out on a date. You are also more likely to act sexual when you are tired or have not been sleeping well. You may also be vulnerable when you are with someone you want to impress with your maturity, or when you are afraid of losing someone you care for.

What do you think about having sex while you're in high school?

I advise bipolar teens against having sex in high school. Bipolar disorder can contribute to impulsivity and poor judgment, and having a sexual relationship at your age can make you vulnerable to emotional injury. I realize that social pressure can be intense if other adolescents in your school are sexually active. Nevertheless, make sure you do not put yourself in a position you will later regret by inviting unwanted pregnancy or sexually transmitted diseases.

What STDs are out there? Am I at extra risk because I'm bipolar?

Some common sexually transmitted diseases (STDs) include gonorrhea, *Chlamydia*, genital warts, and AIDS. Multiple sexual partners are also a risk factor for cervical cancer in women. Bipolar disorder can increase your risk of getting STDs by making your sexual drive unnaturally high, your behavior more impulsive, and your judgment impaired.

Everybody talks about safe sex, but I don't
    know exactly what it means. Tell me.

Sex is called safe when there is no touching between mouth, penis, vagina,
or anus. Diseases can be transmitted when these areas touch, even if no intercourse takes place. Kissing on the mouth is OK.

Is oral sex safe sex?

No. I have had patients who have died of AIDS acquired during oral sex.

What kind of contraceptives are available?
    How are they for bipolar disorder?

Condoms can be purchased everywhere and they provide good protection
from disease and pregnancy. Condoms can be used for protection from oral
sex as well as intercourse.

   All other contraceptives may protect from pregnancy but not disease.
Oral contraceptive pills provide around-the-clock protection from pregnancy,
but only if you remember to take them according to directions and never
run out of pills. Moreover, some oral contraceptive pills contain high doses of
progestins that can cause mood swings and depression in susceptible bipolar girls. If you are considering oral contraceptives, see if your family doctor
or gynecologist can help you minimize progesterone intake.

   Other methods such as rubber diaphragms, contraceptive jelly, foam,
and sponges are inconvenient to use and require prior planning, so they are
of no help for impulsive sex.

11.

CRISIS MANAGEMENT FOR YOUR CHILD AND YOUR FAMILY

. . . .

You will be able to head off crises much better if you and your family can see them coming. If you or your doctor can tell when your child's bipolar disorder is getting worse, you may be able to keep the condition from getting out of control and prevent needless suffering. If the worsening is caused by impulsive actions, such as stopping bipolar medications or using alcohol or other drugs, they can be halted before more damage is done, and prompt treatment will lower your child's likelihood of accidents, self-injury, or suicide. Most important, if conditions do escalate beyond your control, you should know where to go and what to do to make sure your child gets the care that is needed.

My bipolar daughter cries for hours every day and I can't console her. What is going on?

When I hear that a child cries all day long, I think of bipolar depression. Clearly, this is too much sadness for your daughter to bear, and it could be a sign of worsening bipolar disorder. Tell your daughter that you are available any time she wants to talk. Alert her therapist and psychiatrist that her depression may be becoming more severe.

My bipolar son is too emotional right now,
but he has good reasons to feel that way.
What can you do for reasonable emotions
that are causing problems?

Although your son may have good reasons for his emotions, we still do not want him to suffer. Uncontrollable anxiety, ecstasy, fear, despair, hopelessness, jealousy, panic, rage, or sadness are never normal when they are causing problems for your son. If his emotions are particularly vulnerable right now, it could be a sign that his bipolar disorder is getting worse. Just to be on the safe side, contact his doctor and therapist.

My child just paces back and forth all the time.
He can't go to school. What is this?

Ongoing hyperkinesis (too much moving) can be part of manic and mixed states, or be caused by medications. When hyperkinesis appears or worsens suddenly, it may signal an imminent bipolar crisis. Check with your doctor to find out the cause of the pacing and how to treat it. Your child's medications may need to be adjusted.

My son has become completely withdrawn
lately. Could this be worsening bipolar
depression?

Sometimes withdrawal and social isolation can be clues that your son's bipolar depression is getting worse. Your son may stop answering the telephone and stop seeing his friends. He may hole up in his room and refuse to come out. Talk to him and see what is going on. Contact his psychiatrist and see if your child should be evaluated for worsening bipolar disorder.

ꜱHT WARNING SIGNS OF IMPENDING BIPOLAR CRISIS

· · · · · ·

These are some of the things that I look for to help determine whether bipolar disorder is likely to worsen. If several of the items on the list apply to your child, you should be particularly concerned.

1. Increased bipolar symptoms at the time of year when your child usually cycles.
2. A change in sleep (staying up all night or unable to get out of bed and sleeping all day).
3. A change in activity level (either withdrawn and immobile or hyperactive and talking a mile a minute).
4. A change in eating habits with significant weight loss or gain.
5. A change in dress (either disheveled and unwashed, or flamboyant and sexy).
6. Increased anger and irritability, particularly with any signs of violence to self or others.
7. Talking or acting in a way that is not logical or not understandable.
8. Getting in trouble over alcohol or other substance abuse.

Nowadays, my daughter flies into a rage at the least provocation. Is her bipolar disorder getting worse?

Possibly. Anger is a constant companion to children with bipolar disorder and, like other symptoms, irritability increases with stress and physical illness. However, a sudden increase in anger can also be a sign of worsening bipolar disorder or the beginning of a bipolar crisis. Talk to her therapist and psychiatrist to see if they can tell what's going on and whether your child needs to reduce stress and/or have her medications adjusted.

SUICIDAL THOUGHTS AND BEHAVIOR

One study showed that individuals with bipolar disorder have a rate of suicide about thirty times greater than that of the general population. Suicide risks may be even higher in children whose bipolar symptoms start before thirteen years of age. Proper medical treatment greatly reduces your child's risk of suicide attempts and completion.

Does my bipolar depressed daughter have an increased likelihood of suicide?

Your bipolar girl is more likely to commit suicide than her peers. Suicidality can appear with a change of mood or if your daughter were to receive antidepressants. Proper medical treatment is essential here. One study showed that good bipolar treatment could reduce bipolar children's risk of suicide by 75 percent.

Does my bipolar daughter have to be depressed to be suicidal?

Your daughter is vulnerable to suicide at all stages of her bipolar disorder, including bipolar depression, mania, and mixed bipolar disorder. Suicidal risk is worst when children are psychotic, which they may become after taking illegal drugs or antidepressants.

Which bipolar children are at the highest risk for suicide?

Children with alcohol or other drug abuse, numerous hospitalizations, recent stressful life events, and a history of serious medical problems are at a higher risk for suicide. The greatest predictor of future suicide risk is a history of trying to commit suicide in the past.

How can I ask my teenaged bipolar depressed daughter if she is suicidal?

It's best to come right out with it. Sometimes it's easiest just to say "Have you been thinking of killing yourself?" Tell her that you are concerned about how she is feeling and that you do not want to lose her. Your love will touch her and help her want to stay alive.

If she says no, that she has *not* been thinking of taking her life, it shows her that you care and that you want her to be okay. But you may not know if she is suicidal unless you ask.

Will asking my child about suicide make her more likely to kill herself?

The idea of suicide is not a novel one to teenagers, especially depressed teenagers. Most children find it a relief to have an opportunity to unburden their fears and feelings. By asking, you are showing that you want her to live.

How do I know if my son is calling for my help?

When children reveal their suicidal thoughts to you or their professional caretakers, it is a sign that they want help and are willing to work to keep themselves alive.

My bipolar son tried to jump out a window, but we stopped him. What can we do next?

It is time to call the psychiatrist and go to the hospital.

Are there specific medicines that we know can reduce the risk of suicide?

Studies of lithium salt and clozapine show that they can significantly lower the likelihood of suicide. I suspect that other mood stabilizers can also lower suicide risk, but we do not have this data yet.

SOME POSSIBLE PREDICTORS OF SUICIDALITY IN BIPOLAR CHILDREN

- Talking about their death or what the world would be like without them.
- Suddenly developing an unconcerned, bemused, or blasé attitude after being severely depressed.
- Giving away their possessions or talking about who will get their things when they are gone.
- Having no social support network, or withdrawing from friends.
- Losing an important person from their life, by death or separation.
- Hoarding pills in order to have enough to use for suicide.
- Using alcohol or marijuana while in a deep depression.

If your bipolar child has been depressed and you see one or more of these signs, call her psychiatrist and alert him or her to the danger.

BIPOLAR PSYCHOSIS

The nurses where I trained used to refer to psychosis as "poor reality testing" because psychotic people cannot tell what is true and what is false in their own reality. Sometimes professionals use the term psychotic to refer to hallucinations, delusions, distortions, or odd thoughts. One study indicated that more than half of individuals with mania had some psychotic symptoms.

What are hallucinations anyway? How would I know if my bipolar son was having them?

Hallucinations are the experience of visual, auditory, touch, taste, or smell stimuli that are not evident to others. Common visual hallucinations in bipolar disorder include visions of people, destruction, or spiritual experiences. Hearing voices is a common auditory hallucination, but auditory hallucinations can also take the form of a deep humming or droning, a high-pitched hissing, or repeating musical tunes.

What would delusions, distortions, and odd thoughts look like in my bipolar son?

A delusion is a belief in actions and events that are not evident to others. Delusions can include the belief that a conspiracy is afoot, or that your son is being pursued by a member of the Secret Service, FBI, or other elite group. A common sign of bipolar psychosis is the belief that one is close friends with a celebrity. Bipolar psychosis can make it seem that there are special meanings to events or objects. For example, if a psychotic child sees the word "doomed" on an envelope he may believe that he is doomed.

A distortion is a type of delusion based on incorrect interpretation of the available information. For example, your son might see others and be sure that they dislike him because they did not smile at him. Another child may believe that a disappointment is a sign that she will never be happy. Odd thoughts are, well, odd. A bipolar boy once told me sincerely that he was from another planet. A bipolar girl believed that she was really a big plastic doll.

Children are always making up fantasies and playing make-believe. How do you tell the difference?

It seems like it might be difficult to differentiate psychotic experiences from young children's fantasies, but it is usually possible to tell which is which by their extreme content. For example, a girl might have a fantasy that she is a princess while playing. However, if she says that three British men are sending a radioactive beam from the top of the Chrysler Building in New York, telling her that she has to make the sign of the cross whenever she has an impure thought, you can be pretty sure that this is abnormal.

Another clue to the presence of delusions is that most psychotic people aggressively defend the reality of their psychotic experiences. For example, if a child told me that he probably had Native American relatives, I would not doubt him. If a child told me positively that he was a direct relative of

Sitting Bull and that he could prove it, and if he became aggressively defensive and upset at the thought that I might not believe him, I would start to worry.

Does grandiosity play a role in bipolar psychosis?

Delusions are frequently grandiose in content. For example, a psychotic bipolar boy may believe that he has special powers that allow him to control people with his mind. A bipolar girl might believe that she is a well-known celebrity, important spy, party to special secrets, or a confidant of presidents. If she is religious, she may believe that she is a special messenger of God, or that she really *is* either God or the devil.

My son suddenly became psychotic and had to go to the hospital. Are you sure it's bipolar?

Things other than bipolar disorder can trigger sudden, severe psychosis. Large amounts of caffeine, nicotine, marijuana, Salvia, some herbal supplements, and both over-the-counter and prescription drugs can sometimes trigger psychosis in bipolar children. Use of steroid hormones for bodybuilding or taking male hormone supplements can trigger psychosis. Head injury, poisoning, and severe physical illness can also cause psychosis. Drugs such as alcohol, hallucinogens, cocaine, methamphetamine (speed), phencyclidine (PCP), and other stimulants can produce psychotic episodes that are indistinguishable from bipolar psychosis.

What would my child look like if he were psychotic?

On the outside, psychotic children may appear to be looking at or talking to invisible stimuli or talking under their breath to unseen people. They may smile as if they are party to a special secret or they may seem afraid. Bipolar depressive psychosis may produce a complete withdrawal from others to the point that your son does not respond to those around him.

Does the inability to be logical have anything to do with bipolar psychosis?

Frequently bipolar psychosis shows up when children begin to make wildly uncharacteristic decisions and cannot explain themselves. Psychotic individuals may have trouble making themselves understood. There is even a type of bipolar speech called "word salad," in which meaningful words are strung together randomly and make no sense whatsoever.

What effect can worsening bipolar disorder have on my daughter's eating problems?

Bipolar disorder makes it more likely that children with eating problems will develop delusions and hallucinations centered on their weight. Malnourished teens may develop delusional notions that their thin bodies look fat or that their starvation gives them spiritual purity. They may develop the grandiose belief that their emaciated frames are attractive to others. One starving bipolar teen told me, "I can tell everyone is jealous of my thinness. All the men look at me and my body all the time, and I can tell all the women are wishing they were me." In fact, this skeletal teenage girl was in serious medical danger from malnutrition and loss of body tissue. If you see any of these signs, it may signal a need for increased medical care.

My daughter seems to spend all day in a daze, daydreaming. What could this be?

Frequently bipolar depression results in a daydream-y state in which children may lose large chunks of their day. Usually, children tell me they have no thoughts in this state or that they cannot remember their thoughts. Bipolar psychosis can also take this form, where your child is caught up in an internal fantasy that seems like reality. From the outside, this looks like your child is dozing in bed, lying on the couch, or sitting mindlessly in front of the television.

Are the scary voices I am hearing for real? If not, what are they and what can I do for them?

I think that these voices are coming from within your mind as if you were hearing your own thoughts. This process resembles what happens when you are dreaming: you experience things as if they were real, except instead of dreaming you are wide-awake.

First, stop listening to the voices. What they say is pointless. See your doctor to start the process of weaning yourself from these irrelevant voices. In the meantime, it may help to keep your mind busy doing something else.

I heard people talking to *me* on the television. How weird is that?

There are certain experiences called formal thought disorder, which include hearing songs about yourself on the radio, seeing messages about yourself on billboards, or having people on the television turn around and speak directly to you. Formal thought disorder includes the feeling that thoughts are being put in or taken out of your mind, and the experience of having voices describe everything you do. Let me reassure you that this is the bipolar disorder, not your universe falling apart.

Although it seems too simple, many individuals get relief from these scary hallucinations simply by directing their attention somewhere else. Voices can often be rendered ineffectual by humming, whistling, or simply refusing to listen.

I look out and I see a battlefield with people all cut up. What is going on?

I call these "horror movie hallucinations." They are usually images of harm or assault occurring to you or other people. It's like watching a horror movie that has been superimposed on reality. They usually are not lifelike enough that you mistake these images as real, but they can be distracting and disturbing. Fortunately, these images can often be extinguished with a mood stabilizer.

CONDITIONS THAT MAY REQUIRE IMMEDIATE HOSPITALIZATION

It is difficult for parents to deal with bipolar children when their behavior is out of control. To prepare for this contingency, decide what you will do in advance to head off a crisis. The general rule is that immediate hospitalization is necessary if children are likely to hurt themselves or others.

My daughter laughs and says she is okay, but she won't eat or sleep. Help!

Do not take your daughter's word for it; it does not sound like she is okay at all. This could be a sign of worsening bipolar disorder. If you have never seen this behavior before, it could be your daughter's first manic episode. Call and talk to her doctor and therapist. If your daughter's weight gets too low, she may have to go to the hospital.

My son doesn't talk or move or anything! What's wrong?

In severe bipolar disorder, a child may stop moving in a state we call catatonia. This used to be associated with a mental illness called schizophrenia, but we now know that it is usually caused by bipolar disorder. Take your son to his psychiatrist, who may advise hospitalization.

Q My twelve-year-old bipolar depressed
   daughter is hitting and cutting herself.
   What can we do?

This is an intolerable situation, which can result in injury to your daughter. It is also a message from her that something severe is going on inside. Her psychiatrist and therapist may be able to manage this at home, but if there is any serious chance of injury, she may have to go to the hospital. Call your daughter's psychiatrist and let him or her decide.

Q My eight-year-old child is getting violent.
   What can I do so she doesn't hurt
   herself or others?

Call the psychiatrist and follow his or her advice. If you cannot reach the doctor, or you do not like the advice you get, take your child right to the hospital.

Q My son got really angry and hit his father.
   It's just not like him. Is this his bipolar
   disorder?

It is not appropriate for anyone to be violent to their parents or other family members and it can be dangerous if your son is strong. Even if your son is small or easily restrained, this behavior cannot continue. Call your son's doctors; if they decide that your son should stay at home, make sure they tell you what to do if the situation should escalate again. If there is any chance of injury to him or others, extra medications or hospitalization might be necessary to ensure that no one gets hurt.

Q My bipolar child is smashing things, hitting others, and hurting himself. He will not take his medications or go to the doctor. He will not get into the car so I can take him to the hospital. What else can I do?

You have several choices. You can call your doctor or the doctor who is taking their calls and ask him or her to call the hospital to request an ambulance. You can call the hospital directly and ask for an ambulance. Your third option is to call 911 and ask for help. When EMTs and/or officers arrive, they will evaluate your child and the situation to see if they think hospitalization is necessary.

Q How do you decide when the situation is so bad that hospitalization is necessary?

When I start wondering if a child needs to go to the hospital, it is probably the right time for hospitalization.

IN THE HOSPITAL

The hospital is a tool you hold in reserve to help you when the situation becomes too severe to deal with at home. You can prepare yourself by better understanding what hospitalization is all about.

Q What can they do for my son at the hospital that can't be done at home or in the doctor's office?

In the hospital, trained people should be available to watch your son and make sure he does not hurt himself; this alone is important. Being in the hospital can also give your son the opportunity to be seen by several specialists in psychiatry, psychopharmacology, and psychology to advise his regular psychiatrist about new treatment options. Internists and other medical specialists should be available if there are any signs of physical illness complicating the picture. If your son's medications are not working, it is possible to make changes under controlled hospital conditions in the hope of minimizing the stress to your child.

Are there any other benefits you think could come of hospitalizing my son?

When your son is in the hospital, you and the family get a break from the intolerable stress of having a severely ill family member. You will have a chance to talk with each other, to think through your son's role in your family, and to consider how the well-being of your whole family is affected by his illness.

Can I be sure that my child will get all the help he needs in the hospital?

This depends on the size and quality of the hospital, the training and experience of the staff, and how well they do their job together. I have frequently seen children get back on track after a productive hospital stay. However, many hospitals are woefully understaffed at this time, and I have heard some nightmare stories about the treatment at certain hospitals.

What will happen when my daughter and I get to the hospital?

Your daughter may be promptly evaluated and sent to a hospital ward if this is appropriate. Or you and your daughter may have to sit around in an emergency room waiting area for a long time before being seen. Sometimes you can bypass this step by calling your doctor to arrange for your daughter to be preadmitted and taken directly to the hospital.

Under the best conditions, what would happen when my son goes into the hospital?

I have had the privilege to work in some of the best hospitals, and in these settings, psychiatrists and other medical doctors would see your son, a treatment team would discuss your son's diagnosis and individual needs, and orders would be written for his treatment. A nutritionist would meet with him to plan a healthy diet. He would be given medicine by nursing staff who have experience getting children to take their pills without a fight. In addition to medications, your son would receive individual therapy, group therapy, drug abuse–prevention therapy, and occupational therapy. In between therapy sessions, he would participate in activity groups. At the end of your son's treatment, the staff would confirm the next appointment with his outpatient doctor, and a discharge plan would be made to ensure that your son makes the transition from hospital to home smoothly. This is the ideal situation.

What determines the extent of my son's treatment and his length of stay in the hospital?

We would like to believe that your son would get everything he needs when he is hospitalized. However, in the real world, treatment costs, reimbursement, and insurance practices often play significant roles in the extent of your son's treatment and length of stay.

Will my child be able to see her own doctor?

Whether your daughter's current psychiatrist can visit the hospital depends on hospital practices and whether her psychiatrist has or can get privileges at the hospital.

What could make my son's hospital treatment ineffective?

By far, the three main reasons that hospital treatment fails are (1) the diagnosis is wrong; (2) the medications are wrong; (3) the child does not take his medicine.

Our family just doesn't like the hospital doctor. Can we ask to have him changed?

Usually this is possible. Talk to the chief of the hospital ward, or the hospital liaison officer.

We took our child to the hospital, but the place looked gloomy and horrible. Why?

Parents are often disappointed when they step into their bipolar child's hospital ward. Your child's ward may not be allowed to have homey touches like bright pictures on the walls, vases of flowers, lightweight furniture, and floor lamps with power cords, because these objects could prove dangerous in the hands of a depressed or rageful child. Without these decorations, wards look empty and institutional. Add to this the emotional burden of being around so many severely depressed and dysfunctional children, and the experience can be rather dismal.

What can I do to keep my daughter from going back into the hospital?

Talk to her hospital doctors and get their advice on how to keep your daughter healthy. If you find a particularly helpful doctor, you may ask her or him to participate in your daughter's care outside the hospital. Also, talk to the mental health nurses, as they often have great practical experience.

Before your daughter leaves the hospital, talk to the discharge planner and make sure that psychiatry and therapy appointments are ready and waiting when she steps out the door. Talk to the doctor and therapist who will see your daughter outside the hospital and help them develop a plan to keep her healthy after discharge.

Take a good hard look at the level of stress that you and your family, the school, and outside activities are placing on your child. See how much stress can be reduced. Go over her lifestyle and see how it can be healthier. Sometimes the planning done during the last hours before your daughter leaves the hospital can dramatically improve her health after she goes home.

Q My daughter has bipolar disorder that is more severe than most of the patients you talk about. She's always in the hospital, and she has never been out for more than a few weeks in the last two years. How do I help her?

This may be the time for you to fall back and find ways that your daughter can have a good life despite her bipolar symptoms. While your daughter is in the hospital, get help from the social work staff to see if she qualifies for benefits. This can make her eligible for special programs, services, and funds to help her live better with her disorder. Before your daughter is discharged, talk to the discharge planner and find out whether there are outpatient or day-treatment programs available that can help keep her occupied and help her maintain her health. The actual services available will vary widely according to the state and the region.

Talk to your daughter's school and find out what accommodations and considerations are available for your daughter's education. If there are nearby universities with medical schools, check to see if they provide programs and activities for children with mental illness. Frequently you can make your child happier and more stable by ferreting out these options and, by reducing stress, you may make your daughter's illness more stable.

WHAT TO DO WHEN NOTHING IS WORKING

Every parent dreads the possibility that they will run out of options to help their bipolar child. This is a good time to consider what might be missing from your child's treatment.

My daughter has been taking medicine for a year now and there's no improvement. Why?

I see many children who have never been given an opportunity to get well. No matter what other medications your daughter has been given, mood stabilizers are the foundation of bipolar treatment. Check Chapter 5 for more information. You must make sure that she has had an adequate trial of the three major mood stabilizers, carbamazepine, lithium salt, and valproate. Your child should have at least a four-week trial of each of these at therapeutic doses and one trial of two together. Check with your doctor or the *Physicians' Desk Reference (PDR)* to see what doses are recommended for each of the mood stabilizers (see Chapter 12).

My son has gotten worse since we've been buying his medicines from foreign pharmacies. Is there a connection?

Even pharmacies in affluent countries may buy their drugs from cut-rate or unlicensed manufacturing plants in India, the Philippines, or other unexpected locations. These manufacturers are not required to uphold American standards, and the medications they provide may be outdated, too weak, or contaminated with dirt or animal filth. Many counterfeit medications arrive in this country that look like the real products you would buy in your local pharmacy. Instead of the medication you think you are buying, they contain useless fillers. The FDA has even found pills from Internet pharmacies that contain the wrong medications. If your son's health has begun to decline, replace his foreign pills with medications obtained from a local pharmacy you can trust.

My son's not doing well. Is there anything that could be keeping his medications from working?

Smoking cigarettes and drinking grapefruit juice can lower the amount of bipolar medications that reach your son's nervous system. Sometimes infection, injury, and steroid treatment can also work against bipolar medications.

Are there ever any children who cannot be helped by any medication? What do they do?

I have found a few children who are not helped by medications because their bipolar symptoms are too severe, because they have been given inappropriate medications like antidepressants, or because the illness has gone uncontrolled for too long. Some children are so intolerant of medications and their side effects that they cannot take enough to do any good. These children must rely on healthy lifestyle changes to help control their bipolar symptoms until something comes along that works better. We begin by lowering their stress level and keeping it low. We schedule their sleep, meals, and exercise. We make sure their diet contains enough protein and other nutrients. We help avoid stressful outside events that can trigger bipolar symptoms. We do everything we can to make sick children healthier and less vulnerable to bipolar disorder.

What can I do when everything else fails?

Take a break. Clear your head. Check the diagnosis. Look through all the things that can make bipolar disorder worse, including alcohol and other drugs, overexercise, starvation, stress, physical illness, and antidepressants.

ATTITUDES THAT MAKE IT DIFFICULT TO RECOVER FROM BIPOLAR DISORDER

Over the years, I have noticed certain directions of thinking that interfere with recovery. Sometimes these attitudes predict when patients will stop their treatment altogether or when their bipolar disorder is about to flare up. Here are some examples of statements I have heard that reflect these counterproductive attitudes.

1. "I don't think I have bipolar disorder."
2. "My (teacher, friend, grandmother, aunt) doesn't think I have bipolar disorder."
3. "I know a kid who has bipolar disorder and he is nothing like me."
4. "I don't like to think that there is something wrong with me."
5. "Don't mention that 'bipolar' word in front of me. I just want to forget about it."
6. "What I do is my business, not yours."
7. "None of my friends have to take medicine or go to psychotherapy. Why should I?"
8. "Everybody I know drinks and smokes a lot more than I do."
9. "I don't like the doctor anymore."
10. "I don't like the therapist anymore."
11. "I don't need medications. They're what's *making* me sick."
12. "I'm not sick. I don't need to take medications."
13. "I'm not crazy. I don't need psychotherapy."
14. "I don't have a substance problem."
15. "I don't have any problems. The only thing wrong with me is my sleep."
16. "I'm perfectly all right. The only thing that's wrong with me is that I have no friends."
17. "I'm not depressed. I have good reasons to feel the way I do."
18. "I'm perfectly fine. My problems are all caused by (the school, the town, my friends, my family, you)."
19. "Don't worry so much. Trust me. Just wait a while. Things will be okay this time."

What all these attitudes have in common is that they delay, reduce, or derail the treatment of your child's bipolar disorder. It is important not to be sidetracked by these attitudes and to ensure that you, your child's therapist, psychiatrist, and family members form a united front in support of your bipolar child's health.

Make sure your child has been taking his or her medicines, going to the doctor, and participating in therapy sessions. Get a second opinion from a different doctor with specialized training and extra experience. Consider getting an opinion from a well-known doctor in the nearest university hospital. If your current doctor is a family friend, talk to an impartial stranger. Check the Internet for trials of new treatments for bipolar children. Meditate and pray. Stir things up in hopes that the answer will reveal itself.

Bipolar disorder is only beyond hope when we give up.

RESOURCES: USING THE INTERNET TO FIGHT BIPOLAR DISORDER

. . . .

Ultimately, your best source of information will come from working with a psychiatrist and/or therapist who is experienced in treating bipolar disorder and is willing to develop a close working relationship with you. However, there is a wealth of information available to you over the Web, and you should take advantage of it.

Bipolar Web sites offer services such as online support groups, information on local and national meetings, and an opportunity to participate in the politics of health care. They present opportunities to improve your child's health and opportunities for you to help other children. Unfortunately, there is a lot of misleading and incorrect information on the Internet and lots of people with an axe to grind. Start with major societies and institutions that have committed their service to the bipolar community and have no financial, political, or personal profit to be made.

ORGANIZATIONS AND THE SERVICES THEY PROVIDE

Many of the major health organizations work hard to provide services for bipolar sufferers. These Web sites can also be the starting point to join national bipolar organizations, sign up for publications, locate national and statewide conventions, and find local groups.

American Academy of Child and Adolescent Psychiatry (AACAP)

The leading association for child and adolescent psychiatrists is dedicated to treating and improving the quality of life of children, adolescents, and families affected by mental illness.

http://www.aacap.org

http://www.aacap.org/cs/root/about_us/principles_of_practice_of_child_and_adolescent_psychiatry

American Medical Association (AMA)

This is the major organization representing all types of physicians in the United States. It offers information for doctors and patients, and publishes the *Journal of the American Medical Association* (*JAMA*) and the professional psychiatric journal *Archives of General Psychiatry*.

http://www.ama-assn.org

800-621-8335

American Psychiatric Association (APA)

The APA is the premier professional psychiatric society in the United States. Its Web site provides information on psychiatric illnesses and treatment, current news, interest groups, advocacy, and ethics. It publishes the *American Journal of Psychiatry*.

http://www.psych.org

888-357-7924

American Psychiatric Association Alliance

This division of the American Psychiatric Association is dedicated to patients' needs.

http://www.apaalliance.org

American Psychoanalytic Association (APsaA)

This Web site will answer some of your questions about child psychoanalysis.

http://www.apsa.org

American Psychological Association (APA)

Called the "big APA" because there are so many more psychologists than psychiatrists in this country, the American Psychological Association is a vast organization with many services and viewpoints. It promotes psychologists as researchers, testers of bipolar individuals, and psychotherapists to help children improve their cognitive and living skills.

http://www.apa.org/topics/topicbipolar.html

bipolar.com

Pharmaceutical manufacturer GlaxoSmithKline supports this Web site. It features information on recognizing bipolar disorder, treatment, recommended books, and support for families and friends.

http://www.bipolar.com

Bipolar magazine

For twenty dollars, you can purchase a subscription to this quarterly magazine devoted to adults and children with bipolar disorder. Better yet, visit its Web site for free. It contains articles from the printed issues.

http://www.bphope.com

Subscriptions: 888-834-5537

Cbel.com

An index to many professional organizations, articles, private Web pages, and even mailing lists on bipolar disorder.

http://www.cbel.com/mood_disorders

Child and Adolescent Bipolar Foundation

Provides information, message boards, a chat room, and links on childhood bipolar disorder.

www.bpkids.org

Depression and Bipolar Support Alliance (DBSA)

Formerly the National Association for Depression and Manic Depression (NADMD), this organization provides chat rooms, discussion, support groups, speakers, information on advocacy, communication with lawmakers, and an opportunity to share your personal story. It publishes a newsletter called *Outreach*.

http://www.dbsalliance.org

800-826-3632

Feinberg School at Northwestern University

Its Web site provides Nutrition Fact Sheets that explain recommended vitamin doses for children of different ages, as well as the foods that contain them. Look for the site's other fact sheets on minerals and supplements.

http://www.feinberg.northwestern.edu/nutrition/fact-sheets.html

National Alliance on Mental Illness (NAMI)

This organization provides information, support groups, meetings, and information on mental illnesses, including bipolar disorder. It supports public action, advocacy, and demonstrations for the rights of persons with bipolar disorder and other mental illnesses. It also publishes a magazine, *The Advocate*, for members.

http://www.nami.org
www.nami.org/helpline/bipolar-child.html
888-999-6264

PDR Health

A Web site by the people at Thomson Healthcare that presents readable medication information.

http://www.pdrhealth.com

Reality Therapy

Founded in 1967, the William Glasser Institute is a source for information on reality therapy.

http://www.wglasser.com
800-899-0688

Recovery Incorporated

This no-charge, nonprofit, nonsectarian self-help group was founded in 1937 by Abraham A. Low, author of *Mental Health Through Will-Training* (Willett Publishing, Third Edition, 1997). Recovery Incorporated meets in small groups to discuss Dr. Low's book, his methods for controlling emotions and behavior, and how they apply to daily life. Recovery Incorporated has been very helpful for several of my bipolar patients.

http://www.recovery-inc.com
312-337-5661

Stanford University School of Medicine Bipolar Disorders Clinic
A site providing information about bipolar disorder and the treatment programs at my psychiatry alma mater.
http://www.stanford.edu/group/bipolar.clinic/index.html
650-724-4795

World Psychiatric Association (WPA)
This psychiatric society provides international information for professionals and the public. The site contains a useful listing of university departments of psychiatry, hospitals, and mental health organizations around the world.
http://www.wpanet.org

UNITED STATES GOVERNMENT HEALTH AND INFORMATION SERVICES

These federal Web sites contain a huge amount of accurate, useful information. Be prepared to sift through it to find what you want.

ClinicalTrials.gov
This is the official place to learn about new treatments for bipolar disorder. It lists federally and privately supported research studies into new medications, nonmedication treatments, and combinations of existing medications. Just type "bipolar children" in the search box and you will find out about investigations taking place all over the country.
http://www.clinicaltrials.gov

National Institute of Mental Health (NIMH)
This organization distributes information on mental health and mental health research, as well as offering public meetings, advocacy, and access to legislation on mental health issues. This is the real thing.
http://www.nimh.nih.gov
http://www.bipolar.about.com/library/blmisc/bl-nimhchildupdate.htm

NIMH's Psychoactive Drug Screening Program (PDSP) Database
Although it is quite complex, this may be the most remarkable resource on the Web. Here you can find out how every medication works inside the brain. Try entering a value of 1,000 in the box labeled "Ki."

Professor Bryan Roth, M.D., Ph.D.
Department of Pharmacology, University of North Carolina, Chapel Hill, North Carolina
http://kidb.bioc.cwru.edu/pdsp.php

National Institute on Drug Abuse (NIDA)
This Web site shares information and research on drug abuse and addiction from the major government agency devoted to the topic.
http://www.nida.nih.gov

National Mental Health Information Center (NMHIC)
This site features information on protection and advocacy, press releases, and access to information from national publications and libraries.
http://www.mentalhealth.org
800-789-2647

U.S. Food and Drug Administration
The site's Center for Food Safety & Applied Nutrition has a wealth of information about keeping your child healthy. Look for its Food Labeling and Nutrition guide, which tells you what all claims on food labels really mean (http://www.cfsan.fda.gov/~dms/flg-6c.html).
http://www.cfsan.fda.gov/

PRIVATELY OWNED BIPOLAR WEB SITES

There are some great bipolar Web sites out there, waiting to be discovered. This is your opportunity to get help from your peers, check up on the latest controversies, and become part of the international bipolar community.

About.com: Bipolar Children
A page with information, research, blogs, and links about parenting young bipolar children.
http://www.childparenting.about.com/od/bipolardisorder/index.htm

Bipolar Significant Others (BPSO)
A clearinghouse of information for the spouses and caretakers of those with bipolar disorder. You will find a section devoted to children and adolescents.
http://www.bpso.org

Bipolar World: A Bipolar Family
A chatty source of experiences and opinions.
http://www.bipolarworld.net

Brainstorm: Your Pediatric Bipolar InfoSource
A source of support group information. They also have a chat room and a newsletter.
www.bpinfo.net

Dr. Wes Burgess's Web Site
In addition to describing my practice, my Web site contains professional medical articles, as well as notes that I have written on a variety of mental health issues, including bipolar disorder.
http://www.wesburgess.yourMD.com

The Chandler Pamphlet
A descriptive page of information relevant to parents of bipolar children.
http://www.klis.com/chandler/pamphlet/bipolar/bipolarpamphlet.htm

Harbor of Refuge Organization, Inc.
A peer support group for bipolar disorder that offers a chat room, discussion, diet, exercise, and other lifestyle information.
http://www.harbor-of-refuge.org

Juvenile Bipolar Research Foundation
Private supporters of the study of bipolar disorder in children and adolescents.
www.jbrf.org/dvd/index.html

Parenting Bipolar Children
This parent-run Web site offers a support group, a chat room, information, and links.
http://www.parentsofbpkids.freeservers.com

Parents Helping Parents
Parents of children with bipolar disorder share a support group and list bipolar events.
http://www.php.com/include/groups/showInfo.php?ID=58

Patty Duke's Web Site

Patty has shared experiences from her childhood and how it was affected by bipolar disorder and the career expectations placed on a child in the entertainment business.

http://www.pattyduke.com

http://www.pattyduke.blogspot.com

A Silver Lining

A small Web site with a personal touch from others with the disorder, plus a chat room and some adolescent bipolar information.

Their advice on living with bipolar disorder sounds good to me:

1. Accept the fact that we are not weak, that this is a physical illness, which causes mental problems.
2. Have proper prescription and medical management by our psychiatrist and physicians.
3. Avoid stress at all costs.
4. Get proper rest.
5. Continually educate ourselves about our illness.

http://www.a-silver-lining.org

BIPOLAR BLOGS

Blogs and their contents change too often for me to list them here. Instead, I recommend that you type "bipolar blog" into the window of a good search engine like http://www.dogpile.com, http://www. yahoo.com, http://www.blogsearch.google.com, or http://blogs.botw.org. You will find many blogs this way.

PROFESSIONAL BOOKS ON BIPOLAR DISORDER AND MEDICAL SCIENCE

You can find some of the same books that I use for references in university libraries, medical school bookstores, and online. These books are usually expensive, heavy, and so full of medical jargon that they are quite difficult to read, but they contain answers you cannot find anywhere else. Here are some from my bookcase:

Mark Beers, Robert Porter, and Thomas Jones, editors. *The Merck Manual of Diagnosis and Therapy.* John Wiley & Sons, 2006. A reasonably priced medical text with information on all medical conditions for doctors and other medical professionals.

Mark H. Beers, editor. *The Merck Manual of Medical Information.* Simon & Schuster, 2004. The smaller, popular version of the major book on all things medical.

Jerrold G. Bernstein. *Handbook of Drug Therapy in Psychiatry.* C. V. Mosby, 1995. A readable book by the former chair of the Stanford psychiatry department.

F. K. Goodwin and K. Redfield Jamison. *Manic-Depressive Illness.* Oxford University Press, 2007. A collaboration between two experts, one of whom has bipolar disorder.

J. G. Hardman, L. E. Limbird, and A. G. Gilman. *Goodman & Gilman's The Pharmacological Basis of Therapeutics.* McGraw-Hill, 2001. This book provides very deep reading about medications, how they are used, and how they work.

Eric Kandel, J. H. Schwartz, and Thomas M. Jessell. *Principles of Neural Science.* McGraw-Hill, 2000. I think so highly of this book that I used it as a textbook when I taught neuropsychology.

PDR staff, editors. *Physicians' Desk Reference.* Thompson PDR, 2007. More than 3,000 pages of FDA-approved information on many prescription medications, written for physicians.

B. J. Sadock and V. A. Sadock. *Kaplan & Sadock's Comprehensive Textbook of Psychiatry.* Lippincott, Williams & Williams, 2005. The ultimate professional resource on psychiatry facts, theory, and treatment.

GENERAL BOOKS ON BIPOLAR DISORDER FOR PARENTS AND OLDER CHILDREN

These popular books provide an opportunity to discover a variety of different viewpoints on bipolar disorder and related topics.

Tracy Anglada. *Intense Minds.* Trafford Publishing, 2001. This author has combined comments of bipolar children into a unique and useful book.

Wes Burgess, M.D., Ph.D. *The Bipolar Handbook.* Avery, 2006. My previous book answering many questions about adolescent and adult bipolar disorder.

Patty Duke and Gloria Hochman. *A Brilliant Madness.* Bantam Books, 1993. The actress and advocate for bipolar children and adults tells the story of her struggles with bipolar disorder and her miraculous recovery after receiving a mood stabilizer.

Mary Fristad. *Raising a Moody Child.* Guilford Press, 2004. A compendium of helpful information for parents of children suffering from unipolar major depression or bipolar depression.

Patrick Jamieson and Moira Rynn. *Mind Race: A Firsthand Account of One Teenager's Experience with Bipolar Disorder.* Oxford University Press, 2006. A unique, personal story shared by an author who cares deeply about others suffering from bipolar disorder.

Kay Redfield Jamison. *Touched with Fire: Manic-Depressive Illness and the Artistic Temperament.* Touchstone Books, 1996. An important, professionally written book exploring the notion that bipolar disorder is the force behind the greatest creative minds throughout history.

Judith Lederman and Candida Fink. *The Ups and Downs of Raising a Bipolar Child.* Fireside, 2003. A sympathetic and detailed account written by a successful writer and mother of a bipolar child and the psychiatrist and author of the book *Bipolar Disorder for Dummies.*

Francis Mondimore. *Bipolar Disorder.* Johns Hopkins University Press, 1999. A valuable, classic volume addressing symptoms, diagnoses, and treatment by a knowledgeable physician and academic. This book is in the home of many families with bipolar members.

Demitri Papolos and Janice Papolos. *The Bipolar Child: The Definitive and Reassuring Guide to Childhood's Most Misunderstood Disorder.* Broadway Books, 1999, 2002. An impressive and comprehensive classic written by authors actively involved in bipolar education. This book has long been the guiding light for families with bipolar children.

Cindy Singer and Sheryl Gurrentz. *If Your Child Is Bipolar.* Perspective Publishing, 2003. A practical and supportive guide by the woman who founded Mothers with Asperger's Syndrome Kids (M.A.S.K.).

Mitzi Waltz. *Bipolar Disorders: A Guide to Helping Children & Adolescents.* Patient Center Guides, 2000. A comprehensive guidebook to coping successfully with childhood bipolar disorder from the mother of a bipolar adolescent.

RECOMMENDED READING FOR YOUNGER CHILDREN

These calm, loving books teach concern and compassion for all living things. They are meant to be read to small children at bedtime. Meanwhile, the animals act out emotional and social situations that are meaningful to your bipolar child.

Margaret Wise Brown, *Mister Dog,* Little Golden Books, 2003.

Margaret Wise Brown, *Pussy Willow,* Little Golden Books, 1997.

Margaret Wise Brown, *The Sailor Dog,* Little Golden Books, 2001.

Thornton W. Burgess. These wonderful books are back in print by Dover Publications (http://www.doverpublications.com). *The Adventures of Old Mr. Toad* and *Old Mother West Wind* are especially recommended.

Kenneth Grahame, *The Wind in the Willows,* Henry Holt, 2003.

POETRY FOR OLDER READERS

Picking up the reading habit greatly helps children in school and helps broaden a bipolar child's outlook beyond computer, television, text messages, and electronic games. Bipolar readers begin to think about who they are and what they want for their future. In poetry, they can find an outlet for their strong emotions in brief, nonlinear descriptive writing that speaks to the artist in all of us.

e. e. cummings. *95 Poems.* Liverright Publishing, 2002. Cummings continues his bare-bones examination of life as it really is.

T. S. Eliot. *Collected Poems, 1909–1962.* Harcourt, Brace & World, 1991. A lot of bipolar disorder went into the writing of this book.

Margaret Ferguson, Mary Jo Salter, and Jon Stallworthy, editors. *The Norton Anthology of Poetry.* W. W. Norton & Company, 2004. For a poetry-reading girl or boy, this book opens the doorways to a lifetime of adventure.

Edward Fitzgerald, translator. *Omar Khayyam's The Rubayyat of Omar Khayyam.* Kessinger Publishing, 2003. An ancient book beloved by girls and romantics of all ages.

William Keach, editor. *Samuel Taylor Coleridge: The Complete Poems.* Penguin Classics, 1997. Of all poets, I think that Coleridge speaks most strongly with the bipolar voice.

William Shakespeare. S. Orgel and A. R. Braunmuller, editors. *The Complete Pelican Shakespeare.* Penguin Classics, 2002. This book allows the reading child to pick and choose among the bard's best poetry and drama.

MAGAZINES

These magazines stimulate interest in and awareness of many practical lifestyles and careers that can spark excitement in a bipolar child.

Cinefex. Cinefex Publications. This thick quarterly explains what photographers, special-effects artists, computer-graphics specialists, directors, and film producers do in a stunning graphic format showing the work behind the movies. Your child may find himself or herself within these pages.

Fortean Times. Dennis Publications, Limited. An open-minded but critical look at odd phenomena, writers, books, and films.

Maximum PC. Future US, Inc. Inside information about how computer hardware is designed with a slant toward game players.

Popular Science. Bonnier Corporation. This magazine presents an exciting view of the future and how we can make it happen.

PSYCHOLOGICAL AND PHILOSOPHICAL BOOKS

The following books may provide you and older children with some help in describing and dealing with the psychobiological and philosophical aspects of bipolar disorder.

J. Krishnamurti. *Commentaries on Living.* First, Second, and Third Series. Penguin Books, 2006. These readable volumes address a variety of practical issues while demonstrating a philosophy of insight and objectivity.

Robert Pirsig. *Zen and the Art of Motorcycle Maintenance.* HarperCollins, 2006. A practical philosophy set in a story where a man has an emotional (bipolar?) breakdown.

Paul Reps, editor. *Zen Flesh, Zen Bones.* Penguin Books, 2000. Reps has collected material from three books and an article from *Gentry* magazine to illustrate Zen thought. If you are tired of struggling with the rigid, linear Western style of thinking, then you may find this book interesting.

W. H. D. Rouse, editor. *Great Dialogues of Plato.* Signet, 1999. Plato addresses many topics as the mouthpiece of his mentor Socrates, whom some suspect was bipolar.

Manuel Smith. *When I Say No, I Feel Guilty.* Bantam Books, 1985. This classic book will give you an edge in negotiating with the doctor, insurance company, school, and even your children (or parents).

Ludwig Wittgenstein. *Zettel.* G. E. M. Anscombe and G. H. von Wright, editors. University of California Press, 1970. This is a very accessible volume of short thoughts by Wittgenstein on the philosophical outlook that he originated called Logical Positivism.

Author's Disclaimer

Case histories and other patient-related material are made up of a composite of similar cases whose details have been altered so that no example in this book refers to or can be identified with any person, living or dead. The author does not accept money from pharmaceutical corporations, or manufacturers of any medical or health-related products. This book does not constitute an endorsement or recommendation of any products or services mentioned in the text. This book is not a substitute for professional guidance, so please discuss the issues in this book with your doctor. In all cases, use your own best judgment and that of your doctor and therapist to determine which comments in this book will work the most safely and effectively for you and your child.

Appendix 1

THE AMERICAN PSYCHIATRIC ASSOCIATION'S OFFICIAL DIAGNOSTIC CRITERIA FOR BIPOLAR DISORDER

Mania

The *American Psychiatric Association's Diagnostic and Statistical Manual Vol. IV, Text Revision (DSM-IV-TR)* diagnostic criteria for mania include:

A. A distinct period of abnormally and persistently elevated, expansive, and/or irritable mood, lasting at least one week (or any duration if hospitalization is necessary).

B. During the period of mood disturbance, three (or more) of the following symptoms have persisted (four if the mood is only irritable) and have been present to a significant degree:

Inflated self-esteem or grandiosity

A decreased need for sleep (e.g., feels rested after only three hours of sleep)

More talkative than usual or pressure to keep talking

Flight of ideas or subjective experience that thoughts are racing

Distractibility (i.e., attention too easily drawn to unimportant or irrelevant external stimuli)

Increase in goal-directed activity (either socially, at work, in school, or sexually) or psychomotor agitation

Excessive involvement in pleasurable activities that have a high potential for painful consequences (e.g., engaging in unrestrained buying sprees, sexual indiscretions, or foolish business investments).
C. The symptoms do not meet criteria for a Mixed Bipolar Episode.
D. The mood disturbance is sufficiently severe to cause marked impairment in occupational functioning or in usual social activities or relationships with others or to necessitate hospitalization to prevent harm
to self or others, or there are psychotic features.
E. The symptoms are not due to the direct physiological effects of a
substance (e.g., a drug of abuse, a medication, or other treatment) or
a general medical condition (e.g., hyperthyroidism).

Depression

The *American Psychiatric Association's Diagnostic and Statistical Manual Vol. IV,
Text Revision (DSM-IV-TR)* diagnostic criteria for depression with atypical
features include:

Atypical features can be applied when these features predominate during
the most recent two weeks of a current Major Depressive Episode in Major
Depressive Disorder or in Bipolar I or Bipolar II Disorder when a current
Major Depressive Episode is the most recent type of mood episode, or when
these features predominate during the most recent type of mood episode,
or when these features predominate during the most recent two years of
Dysthymic Disorder; if the Major Depressive Episode is not current, it ap-
plies if these features predominate during any two-week period.

A. Mood reactivity (i.e., mood brightens in response to actual or potential
positive events).
B. Two (or more) of the following features:
Significant weight gain or increase in appetite
Hypersomnia
Leaden paralysis (i.e., heavy, leaden feelings in arms or legs)
Long-standing pattern of interpersonal rejection sensitivity (not limited
to episodes of mood disturbance) that results in significant social
or occupational impairment
C. Criteria are not met for Depression with Melancholic Features or
Depression with Catatonic Features during the same episode.

Reprinted with permission from the *Diagnostic and Statistical Manual of
Mental Disorders,* Fourth Edition, Text Revision (Copyright 2000), American
Psychiatric Association.

Appendix 2

THE NATIONAL INSTITUTE OF MENTAL HEALTH'S SYMPTOMS OF MANIA, GENERAL DEPRESSION, AND PSYCHOSIS

Signs and symptoms of *mania* include:

- Increased energy, activity, and restlessness
- Excessively "high," overly good, euphoric mood
- Extreme irritability
- Racing thoughts and talking very fast, jumping from one idea to another
- Distractibility, can't concentrate well
- Little sleep needed
- Unrealistic beliefs in one's abilities and powers
- Poor judgment
- Spending sprees
- A lasting period of behavior that is different from usual
- Increased sexual drive
- Abuse of drugs, particularly cocaine, alcohol, and sleeping medications
- Provocative, intrusive, or aggressive behavior
- Denial that anything is wrong

A manic episode is diagnosed if elevated mood occurs with three or more of the other symptoms most of the day, nearly every day, for one week or longer. If the mood is irritable, four additional symptoms must be present.

Signs and symptoms of *general* [bipolar and unipolar] *depression* include:

- Lasting sad, anxious, or empty mood
- Feelings of hopelessness or pessimism
- Feelings of guilt, worthlessness, or helplessness
- Loss of interest or pleasure in activities once enjoyed, including sex
- Decreased energy, a feeling of fatigue or of being "slowed down"
- Difficulty concentrating, remembering, making decisions
- Restlessness or irritability
- Sleeping too much, or can't sleep
- Change in appetite and/or unintended weight loss or gain
- Chronic pain or other persistent bodily symptoms that are not caused by physical illness or injury
- Thoughts of death or suicide, or suicide attempts

A depressive episode is diagnosed if five or more of these symptoms last most of the day, nearly every day, for a period of two weeks or longer.

Common symptoms of *psychosis* include:

- Hallucinations: hearing, seeing, or otherwise sensing the presence of things not actually there
- Delusions: false, strongly held beliefs not influenced by logical reasoning or explained by a person's usual cultural beliefs

Psychotic symptoms in bipolar disorder tend to reflect the extreme mood state at the time. For example, delusions of grandiosity, such as believing that one is the president or has special powers or wealth, may occur during mania; delusions of guilt or worthlessness, such as believing that one is ruined and penniless or has committed some terrible crime, may appear during [unipolar major] depression. People with bipolar disorder who have [psychotic] symptoms are sometimes incorrectly diagnosed as having schizophrenia, another severe mental illness.

Reprinted with permission from the National Institute of Mental Health. Bipolar disorder, http://www.nimh.nih.gov/publicat/bipolar.cfm, Bethesda, MD: National Institute of Mental Health, National Institutes of Health, U.S. Department of Health and Human Services; 2001. Updated: 09/02/2005. NIH Publication No. 3679.

Index